Clar

May, 1962

JOSEF PIEPER

FORTITUDE
AND
TEMPERANCE

translated by
Daniel F. Coogan

PANTHEON BOOKS

Copyright 1954 by Pantheon Books Inc.
333 Sixth Avenue, New York 14, N.Y.
Library of Congress Catalogue Card Number: 53-9948

Original German Titles:
Vom Sinn der Tapferkeit
and
Zucht und Mass

NIHIL OBSTAT:

MARTINUS J. HEALY, S.T.D.

CENSOR LIBRORUM

IMPRIMATUR:

✠ THOMAS EDMUNDUS MOLLOY, S.T.D.

ARCHIEPISCOPUS-EPISCOPUS

BROOKLYNIENSIS

Brooklynii, die iv Januarii 1954

Manufactured in the U.S.A.
American Book–Stratford Press, Inc., New York

CONTENTS

FORTITUDE

TEMPERANCE

FORTITUDE

THE THIRD CARDINAL VIRTUE

"The praise of fortitude is dependent upon justice." St. Thomas Aquinas

1. INTRODUCTION

AN ERRONEOUS or defective interpretation of the reality of existence inevitably gives rise to false goals and faulty ideals. For, as all things should be grounded in being, so must the guideposts of action be rooted in the knowledge of reality.

True to this general law, enlightened liberalism—this widespread and intricate, yet fundamentally uniform network of misinterpretations of the objective reality of man, which has stamped with its distinctive mark the century now gradually fading into the irretrievable past —inevitably produced a disastrous distortion of the idea of ethical man. This distortion falsifies and deprives of their reality the very concepts in which Western Christianity has come to summarize the due and proper image of man: prudence, justice, fortitude, and temperance.

It is true that all four cardinal virtues have been debased in the liberal's concept of man; but quite specifically it is the original significance of the virtues of fortitude and temperance which has eluded him. His secularized, bourgeois optimism made it impossible for the liberal to penetrate to the true basis of these two virtues. Their foundation in reality, without which neither forti-

9

tude nor temperance can be thought of significantly as virtues, is the metaphysical fact of the existence of evil: evil in the world of men, evil in the world of spirits; evil in the twofold form of guilt and punishment; that is, the evil that we do, and the evil that we suffer.[1] The things that prevent the enlightened liberal from knowing and above all acknowledging, this fundamental reality are his resolute worldliness together with his unbounded earthly optimism, and, as the product of these two, his middle-class metaphysics. Anxiously bent on security he "desires to remain exempt from fortitude."[2] Natural reason only inadequately apprehends the dark essential core of sin. Faith alone is aware of the mysterious chasm of creaturely guilt. (The supernatural order establishes not only higher possibilities of happiness, but also more abysmal depths of sadness.) To a purely "natural" optimism and to a tense and stubborn preoccupation with security, the teaching of the Church that, through original sin, "natural man" (that is, the man who is not attached to Christ) is definitely "under the dominion of Satan," becomes suddenly and compellingly evident only when both these attitudes cancel each other out.

The virtue of temperance and moderation is conceivable only on the basis of the fact that man has lost, together with his original sanctity, his *integritas*, his "intactness," the self-evident inner order of his nature. Only on the premise that an unnatural revolt of the subordinate powers of the soul against the rule of the spirit is possible and recognized as possible, can "moderation" be conceived of as a virtue. Liberalism's denial or disregard of this premise could not but lead to an undermining of the genuine ethical significance of "temperance." By contrast, there developed, especially in the "Christian middle classes," an unsound overvaluation of moderation, to the point that modern usage has confined the notion of "morality" almost exclusively to this partial area. As a result of this middle-class exteriorization of this virtue, the word "morality" has acquired an ironic and derogatory connotation. This overvaluation of the restraining fight against inordinate passion, this confinement of the ethical to the private sphere, quite obviously originates in the spirit of individualism. The classical theology of the Church ranks temperance as the last and lowest of the cardinal virtues, for the express reason that it relates solely to the individual man.[3] This, of course, implies no prejudice against the shining pre-eminence of chastity, nor a denial of the ignominy of undisciplined license.

The power of evil is manifested in its fearfulness. To fight against this fear-inspiring power—by endurance as well as by attack—is the function of fortitude, which Augustine asserts to be an "incontrovertible witness" for the existence of evil.[4]

Enlightened liberalism closes its eyes to the evil in the world: to the demonic power of "our adversary" the Devil, the Evil One, as well as to the mysterious power of human delusion and perversion of will; at worst, the liberal imagines the power of evil to be not so "gravely" dangerous that one could not "negotiate" or "come to terms" with it. The uncomfortable, merciless and inexorable "No," a self-evident reality to the Christian, has been obliterated from the liberalistic world view. The ethical life of man has become falsified into an unheroic, unthreatened way of existence free from sorrow and harm; the way to perfection has come to appear as a plant-like "unfolding" and "growth," succeeding without effort in attaining the good.

By contrast, the cornerstone of Christian ethical teaching is the concept of the *bonum arduum*, the "steep good," beyond the reach of the easy grasp. To liberalism, genuine fortitude, exerting itself in vital struggle, must appear senseless, the valiant man a simpleton. On the other hand, liberalism has brought in its wake, as its consequence and as a protest, a fortitude which boldly claims the wreath of heroism simply for blind "sacrifice" and self-surrender, regardless to what end.

In what follows, we shall make an effort to disclose the true significance of human fortitude as a virtue, that is, its *Christian* significance.

It would, of course, be of little value to advance private opinions on the Christian significance of fortitude. Christian truth is in its origin and primarily in the custody of the teaching office of the Church; the individual possesses it only when he lives in union with the Church and hearkens by faith to her teaching. Accordingly, this excursus makes no claim whatever to originality of thought. Rather, it contains not a single sentence that could not be documented from the works of St. Thomas Aquinas, the "Universal Doctor" of the Church.

II. READINESS TO FALL IN BATTLE

FORTITUDE presupposes vulnerability; without vulnerability there is no possibility of fortitude. An angel cannot be brave, because he is not vulnerable. To be brave actually means to be able to suffer injury. Because man is by nature vulnerable, he can be brave.

By injury we understand every assault upon our natural inviolability, every violation of our inner peace; everything that happens to us or is done with us against our will; thus everything in any way negative, everything painful and harmful, everything frightening and oppressive.

The ultimate injury, the deepest injury, is death. And even those injuries which are not fatal are prefigurations of death; this extreme violation, this final negation, is reflected and effective in every lesser injury.

Thus, all fortitude has reference to death. All fortitude stands in the presence of death. Fortitude is basically readiness to die, or more accurately: readiness to fall, to die, in battle.

Every injury to the natural being is fatal in its intention. Thus every courageous action has as its deepest root the readiness to die, even though, viewed from without, it may appear entirely free from any thought of death. Fortitude that does not reach down into the depths of the willingness to die is spoiled at its root and devoid of effective power.

Readiness proves itself in taking a risk, and the culminating point of fortitude is the witness of blood. The essential and the highest achievement of fortitude is martyrdom, and readiness for martyrdom is the essential root of all Christian fortitude. Without this readiness there is no Christian fortitude.

An age that has obliterated from its world view the notion and the actual possibility of martyrdom must necessarily debase fortitude to the level of a swaggering gesture. One must not overlook, however, that this obliteration can be effected in various ways. Next to the timid opinion of the philistine that truth and goodness "prevail of themselves," without demanding any personal commitment, there is the equally pernicious easy enthusiasm which never wearies of proclaiming its "joyful readiness for martyrdom." In both cases, the witness of blood is equally bereft of reality.

The Church thinks otherwise on this matter. On the one hand she declares: Readiness to shed one's blood for Christ is imposed by the strictly binding law of God. "Man must be ready to let himself be killed rather than to deny Christ or to sin grievously."[1] Readiness to die is therefore one of the foundations of Christian life. But as regards a garrulous enthusiasm for martyrdom, let us see what the Church of the martyrs thought about it. In the "Martyrdom of St. Polycarp," one of the oldest accounts from the period of persecution (about A.D. 150), sent by the "Church of God in Smyrna" to "all congregations of the holy and Catholic Church," a brief paragraph is explicit:

> "But one, a Phrygian called Quintus, became afraid when he saw the wild animals. It was this very man who had presented himself voluntarily to the court and persuaded others to do the same. By repeated urging the Proconsul brought him to sacrifice and to forswear Christ. Therefore, brethren, we have no praise for those who offer themselves voluntarily; this is not the counsel of the Gospel."[2]

The Church Father St. Cyprian, who was beheaded in 258, declared to the Consul Paternus: "Our teaching forbids anyone to report himself."[3] It appears that the Fathers of the ancient Church, from St. Cyprian to St. Gregory of Nazianz and St. Ambrose, actually assumed that God would most readily withdraw the strength of endurance from those who, arrogantly trusting their own resolve, thrust themselves into martyrdom. St. Thomas Aquinas finally, in whose *Summa* an article deals with the so-called "joys of fortitude," says that the pain of martyrdom obscures even the spiritual joy in an act pleasing to God, "unless the overflowing grace of God lift the soul with exceeding strength to things divine."[4]

In the face of the unromantic, harsh reality expressed

in these grave statements, all bombastic enthusiasm and oversimplification vanish into thin air. In this, then, does the actual significance of the unyielding fact that the Church counts readiness to shed one's blood among the foundations of Christian life become clearly manifest.

The suffering of injury is only a partial and foreground aspect of fortitude. The brave man suffers injury not for its own sake, but rather as a means to preserve or to acquire a deeper, more essential intactness.

Christian consciousness has never lost the certainty that an injury suffered in fighting for the good confers an intactness which is more closely and intimately related to the core of man's life than all purely natural serenity, though critics and opponents of Christianity have not always succeeded in recognizing and correctly estimating either this certainty or its rank among Christian vital forces.

To the early Church, martyrdom appeared as a victory, even though a fatal one. "He conquers for the Faith by his death; living without the Faith he would be conquered,"[5] says St. Maximus of Turin, a bishop of the fifth century, concerning the witness of blood. And in Tertullian we read: "We are victorious when we are stricken down; we escape when we are led before the judge."[6]

The fact that these victories are fatal or at least harmful belongs to the incomprehensible and immutable conditions under which the Christian—and perhaps not only he—exists in the world. Thomas Aquinas seems to consider it to be almost the nature of fortitude that it fights against the *superior* power of evil, which the brave man can defeat only by his death or injury. We shall take up this thought again later.

First and foremost: the brave man does not suffer injury for its own sake. For the Christian no less than for the "natural" man, "suffering for its own sake" is nonsense. The Christian does not despise the things that are destroyed by injury. The martyr does not simply consider life of little worth, though he does value it cheaper than that for which he sacrifices it. The Christian loves his life, says Thomas, not only with the natural, life-asserting forces of the body, but with the moral forces of the spiritual soul as well. Nor is this said by way of apology. Man loves his natural life not because he is "a mere man"; he loves it because and to the extent that he is a *good* man.[7] The same applies not only to life itself, but to everything included in the range of natural intactness: joy, health, success, happiness. All these things are genuine goods, which the Christian does not toss aside and esteem but lightly—unless, indeed, to preserve higher goods, the loss of which would injure more deeply the inmost core of human existence.

The validity of all this is not impaired by the fact that obviously the heroic life of the saints and great Christians is far more than the result of a carefully calculated reckoning of profit and loss.

17

III. FORTITUDE MUST NOT TRUST ITSELF

IF THE SPECIFIC CHARACTER of fortitude consists in suffering injuries in the battle for the realization of the good, then the brave man must first know what the good is, and he must be brave for the sake of the good. "It is for the sake of the good that the brave man exposes himself to the danger of death."[1] "In overcoming danger, fortitude seeks not danger itself, but the realization of rational good."[2] "To take death upon oneself is not in itself praiseworthy, but solely because of its subordination to good."[3] It is not the injury that matters primarily, but the realization of the good.

Therefore fortitude, though it puts man to the severest test, is not the first and greatest of the virtues. For neither difficulty nor effort causes virtue, but the good alone.[4]

Fortitude therefore points to something prior. Essentially it is something secondary, subordinate, deriving its measure from something else. It has its place in a scale of meaning and value where it does not rank first. Fortitude is not independent, it does not stand by itself. It receives its proper significance only in relation to something other than itself.

"Fortitude must not trust itself," says Ambrose.[5]

Every child knows that in the list of cardinal virtues fortitude comes third. This enumeration is not accidental: it is a meaningfully graded series.

Prudence and justice precede fortitude. And that means, categorically: without prudence, without justice, there is no fortitude; only he who is just and prudent can also be brave; to be really brave is quite impossible without at the same time being prudent and just also.

Nor is it possible to discuss the nature of fortitude without examining its relation to prudence and justice.

To begin with, only the prudent man can be brave. Fortitude without prudence is not fortitude.

The growing surprise we experience as we examine this proposition more closely marks the measure of our estrangement from the self-evident foundations of the classical teachings of the Church on human life. Only recently have we hesitantly begun to rediscover what is expressed in this proposition, namely, the proper place and the high rank that belong to prudence.

To mention fortitude and prudence in the same breath seems in a measure to contradict modern man's notion of prudence and also of fortitude. This is partially due to the fact that current usage does not designate quite the same thing by "prudence" as classical theology understood by *prudentia* and *discretio*. The term "prudence" has come to mean rather the slyness which permits the cunning and "shrewd" tactician to evade any dangerous risk to his person, and thus escape injury and even the possibility of injury. To us, prudence seems to be that false "discretion" and "cool consideration" conjured up by the coward in order to be able to shirk the test. To "prudence" thus conceived, fortitude seems plainly unwise or stupid.

Prudence has a double aspect. One side is concerned with gathering knowledge, with establishing a yardstick, and is directed toward reality; the other side is concerned with decision and command, with evaluation, and is directed toward will and action. In the former, the truth of things finds its reflection; in the latter, the norm of action becomes evident.

The relation of prudence to reality must by its nature precede the relation to action. Prudence "translates"— by cognition and direction—the truth of real things into the goodness of human activity. And only in this is human activity objectively good: that it can be "retranslated" into true knowledge of things. Sin is always (though not exclusively!) based also on an erroneous judgment of the nature of things.

Thus prudence does not simply rank first in the scale of cardinal virtues, it actually is the "mother of virtues,"[6] and "gives birth" to the others; it is the inner form of the other virtues, as the soul is the inner form of the body.[7] The first thing required of the active man is that he have some knowledge of reality, namely a directive knowledge, a knowledge referable to action; this "directive knowledge" constitutes the essential part of prudence.[8] "All moral virtue must be prudent."[9] Without prudence there is neither justice nor fortitude nor moderation. All three exist through prudence.

Fortitude therefore becomes fortitude through being "in-formed" by prudence. The double meaning of "inform" is here very apt. "Inform" in the current usage means primarily "instruct"; secondly, as a technical term of scholasticism, taken directly from the Latin *informare*, it means "to give inner form to." Referring to the relation between prudence and fortitude, the two meanings interlock: in the instruction of fortitude by prudence the former receives from the latter its inner form, that is, its specific character as a virtue.

The virtue of fortitude has nothing to do with a purely vital, blind, exuberant, daredevil spirit. (On the other hand it presupposes a healthy vitality, perhaps more than any other virtue.) The man who recklessly and indiscriminately courts any kind of danger is not for that reason brave; all he proves is that, without preliminary examination or distinction, he considers all manner of things more valuable than the personal intactness which he risks for their sake.[10] The nature of fortitude is not determined by risking one's person arbitrarily, but only by a sacrifice of self in accordance with reason, that is, with the true nature and value of real things. "Not in any way whatsoever, but according to reason."[11] Genuine fortitude presupposes a correct evaluation of things, of the things that one risks as well as of those which one hopes to preserve or gain by the risk.

Pericles, in the lofty words of his speech for the fallen heroes, expressed Christian wisdom also: "For this too is our way: to dare most liberally where we have reflected best. With others, only ignorance begets fortitude; and reflection but begets hesitation."[12]

Prudence gives their inner form to all the other cardinal virtues: justice, fortitude, and moderation. But these three are not equally dependent upon prudence. Fortitude is less directly informed by prudence than justice; justice is the first word of prudence, fortitude the second; prudence informs fortitude, as it were, through justice. Justice is based solely upon the recognition of reality achieved by prudence; fortitude, however, is based upon prudence and justice together.

Thomas Aquinas gives the following explanation for the hierarchy of the cardinal virtues: the actual good of man is his self-realization in accordance with reason, that is, in accordance with the truth of real things. (Let us keep in mind that for the classical theology of the Church, reason always and only means the "passage" to reality. We must avoid the temptation of transferring our justifiably contemptuous lack of confidence in the dictatorial "reason" of the idealist philosophers of the nineteenth century to the *ratio* of scholasticism, always closely related to reality.) The essence of this "good of reason" is conferred in the directive cognition of prudence. In the virtue of justice, this good of reason becomes transformed into actual existence. "It is the function of justice to carry out the order of reason in all

human affairs." The other virtues—fortitude and moderation—serve the conservation of this good; it is their function to preserve man from declining from the good.
Among these two latter virtues, fortitude takes prece-
dence.[13]

Under the direction of prudence, the good of man
becomes compellingly evident. Justice primarily brings
about the actual realization of this good. Fortitude therefore, by itself, is not the primary realization of the good.
But fortitude protects this realization or clears the road
for it.

So we cannot simply say that only the prudent man
can be brave. We have further to see that a "fortitude"
which is not subservient to justice is just as false and un-
real as a "fortitude" which is not informed by prudence.

Without the "just cause" there is no fortitude. "Not
the injury, but the cause makes martyrs," says St. Augustine.[14] "Man does not expose his life to mortal danger,
except to maintain justice. Therefore the praise of fortitude depends upon justice," says St. Thomas.[15] And in his
Book of Duties, St. Ambrose says: "Fortitude without
justice is a lever of evil."[16]

IV. ENDURANCE AND ATTACK

To BE BRAVE is not the same as to have no fear. Indeed, fortitude actually rules out a certain kind of fearlessness, namely the sort of fearlessness that is based upon a false appraisal and evaluation of reality. Such fearlessness is either blind and deaf to real danger, or else it is the result of a perversion of love. For fear and love depend upon each other: a person who does not love, does not fear either, and he who loves falsely, fears falsely. One who has lost the will to live does not fear death. But this indifference to life is far removed from genuine fortitude; it is, indeed, an inversion of the natural order. Fortitude recognizes, acknowledges, and maintains the natural order of things. The brave man is not deluded: he sees that the injury he suffers is an evil. He does not undervalue and falsify reality; he "likes the taste" of reality as it is, real; he does not love death nor does he despise life. Fortitude presupposes in a certain sense that man is afraid of evil; its essence lies not in knowing no fear, but in not allowing oneself to be forced into evil by fear, or to be kept by fear from the realization of good.

Whoever exposes himself to a danger—even for the

sake of good—without knowledge of its perils, either from instinctive optimism ("nothing can possibly happen to *me*") or from firm confidence in his own natural strength and fighting fitness, does not on that account possess the virtue of fortitude.[1]

It is possible to be genuinely brave only when all those real or apparent assurances fail, that is, when the natural man is afraid; not, however, when he is afraid out of unreasoning timidity, but when, with a clear view of the real situation facing him, he cannot help being afraid, and, indeed, with good reason. If in this supreme test, in face of which the braggart falls silent and every heroic gesture is paralyzed, a man walks straight up to the cause of his fear and is not deterred from doing that which is good; if, moreover, he does so for the sake of good— which ultimately means for the sake of God, and therefore not from ambition or from fear of being taken for a coward—this man, and he alone, is truly brave.

To maintain this position is not to depreciate in the least the value of natural optimism and natural strength and fighting fitness; neither is their vital significance or their great ethical importance thereby diminished. It is, however, important to understand wherein lies the actual nature of fortitude as a virtue, and to realize that it lies beyond the realm of the merely vital. In the face of martyrdom, all natural optimism becomes senseless, and the hands of the man most fit for battle are, literally, tied. But as martyrdom is the essential and the highest achievement of fortitude, it is only in this supreme test that its true nature stands revealed and the yardstick for its less heroic realizations is provided (for it belongs to the nature of virtue to fix its gaze upon the ultimate).[2]

Fortitude consequently does not mean mere fearlessness. That man alone is brave who cannot be forced, through fear of transitory and lesser evils, to give up the greater and actual good, and thereby bring upon himself that which is ultimately and absolutely dreadful. This fear of the ultimately dreadful belongs, as the "reverse" of the love of God, to the absolutely necessary foundations of fortitude (and of all virtue): "He who feareth the Lord will tremble at *nothing*" (Eccli. 34:16).

So whoever realizes the good by facing what is dreadful, by facing injury, is truly brave. This "facing" the dreadful has two aspects, which form the foundation for the two basic acts of fortitude: endurance and attack.

Endurance is more of the essence of fortitude than attack. This proposition of St. Thomas[3] may seem strange to us, and many of our contemporaries may glibly dismiss it as the expression of a "typically medieval" "passivist" philosophy and doctrine. Such an interpretation, however, would hit wide of the mark. Thomas in no way means to rate endurance in itself higher than attack, or to propose that in every case it is braver to endure than to attack. What, then, does his proposition mean? It can mean only that the true "position" of fortitude is that extremely perilous situation described above, in which to suffer and endure is objec-

26

tively the only remaining possibility of resistance, and that it is in this situation that fortitude primarily and ultimately proves its genuine character. It is of course an integral part of St. Thomas' conception of the world, of the Christian conception of the world, that man may be placed in a position to be injured or killed for the realization of the good and that evil, considered in terms of this world, may appear as an overwhelming power. This possibility, we know, has been obliterated from the world-view of enlightened liberalism.

To suffer and endure is, furthermore, something passive only in an external sense. Thomas himself raises the objection: if fortitude is a perfection, then how can enduring be its essential act? For enduring is pure passivity, and active doing is more perfect than passive suffering. And he replies: enduring comprises a strong activity of the soul, namely, a vigorous grasping of and clinging to the good; and only from this stout-hearted activity can the strength to support the physical and spiritual suffering of injury and death be nourished.[4] It cannot be denied that a timid Christianity, overwhelmed and frightened by the un-Christian criteria of an ideal of fortitude that is activistically heroic, has smothered this fact in the general consciousness, and misconstrued it in the sense of a vague and resentful passivism.

The same applies, and even to a higher degree, to the current notion of the virtue of patience. For Thomas, patience is a necessary component of fortitude. We are apt to regard this coordination of patience with fortitude as incongruous, not only because we easily mistake the nature of fortitude for activism, but first and foremost because in our conception patience (in sharp contrast to the ideas of classical theology) has come to mean an indiscriminate, self-immolating, crabbed, joyless and spineless submission to whatever evil is met with, or worse, deliberately sought out. Patience, however, is something quite other than the indiscriminate acceptance of any and every evil: "The patient man is not the one who does not flee from evil, but the one who does not allow himself to be made inordinately sorrowful thereby."[5] To be patient means to preserve cheerfulness and serenity of mind in spite of injuries that result from the realization of the good. Patience does not imply the exclusion of energetic, forceful activity, but simply, explicitly and solely the exclusion of sadness and confusion of heart.[6] Patience keeps man from the danger that his spirit may be broken by grief and lose its greatness.[7] Patience, therefore, is not the tear-veiled mirror of a "broken" life (as one might easily assume in the face of what is frequently presented and praised under this name), but the radiant embodiment of ultimate integrity. In the words of Hildegard of Bingen, patience is "the pillar which nothing can soften."[8] And Thomas, following Holy Scripture (Luke 21:19), summarizes with superb precision: "Through patience man possesses his soul."[9]

The man who is brave is for that very reason patient as well. But the reverse proposition cannot be said to be true: patience by itself does not constitute the whole of fortitude,[10] no more, nay, less than does endurance, to which patience is subordinated. The brave man not only knows how to bear inevitable evil with equanimity; he will also not hesitate to "pounce upon" evil and to bar its way, if this can reasonably be done. This attitude requires readiness to attack, courage, self-confidence, and hope of success; "the trust that is a part of fortitude signifies the hope which a man puts in himself: naturally in subordination to God."[11] These things are so self-evident that we need not waste words upon them.

The fact, however, that Thomas assigns to (just) wrath a positive relation to the virtue of fortitude has become largely unintelligible and unacceptable to present-day Christianity and its non-Christian critics. This lack of comprehension may be explained partly by the exclusion, from Christian ethics, of the component of passion (with its inevitably physical aspect) as something alien and incongruous—an exclusion due to a kind of intellectual stoicism—and partly by the fact that the explosive activity which reveals itself in wrath is naturally repugnant to good behavior regulated by "bourgeois" standards. So Thomas, who is equally free from both these errors, says: The brave man uses wrath for his own act, above all in attack, "for it is peculiar to wrath to pounce upon evil. Thus fortitude and wrath work directly upon each other."[12]

Not only as regards the "passive," but also as regards the pronouncedly "aggressive," the classical doctrine of fortitude exceeds the narrow range of conventional notions.

Yet the fact remains that that which is preponderantly of the essence of fortitude is neither attack nor self-confidence nor wrath, but endurance and patience. Not because (and this cannot be sufficiently stressed) patience and endurance are in themselves better and more perfect than attack and self-confidence, but because, in the world such as it is constituted, it is only in the supreme test, which leaves no other possibility of resistance than endurance, that the inmost and deepest strength of man reveals itself. Power is so manifestly of the very structure of the world that endurance, not wrathful attack, is the ultimately decisive test of actual fortitude, which, essentially, is nothing else than to love and to realize that which is good, in the face of injury or death, and undeterred by any spirit of compromise. It is one of the fundamental laws of a world plunged into disorder by original sin that the uttermost strength of the good manifests itself in powerlessness. And the Lord's words, "Behold, I send you as sheep among wolves" (Matt. 10:16), continue to mark the position of the Christian in the world, even to this day.

This thought and this reality may appear virtually unacceptable to each "new generation." The reluctance to acknowledge them and the inner revolt against the "resignation" of those who have "resigned themselves" are, indeed, hallmarks of genuine youthfulness. In this revolt, at least, there lives the ineradicable human sense of the original and essential order of creation, an intimation that no genuine Christian can lose, even though he has learned to acknowledge the spiritually inevitable disorder caused by original sin, not only as an idea to be conceived, but as a reality to be experienced. Implicit in the aforesaid is the fact that there are also non-Christian or pre-Christian modes of "putting up with" which it may be the perpetual mission of youth to overcome, and specifically of Christian youth.

Further: the figure of the "sheep among wolves" refers above all to the hidden depth of Christian existence in the world, although, as an actual possibility, it forms the foundation of all concrete conflicts, determining and coloring them all. It is disclosed in its naked and absolute reality, however, only in cases of the supreme test; then, indeed, the pure and unadulterated realization of this figure is demanded of every Christian. On the surface, above this depth, there lies the broad field of active worldly endeavor and the struggle for the realization of the good against the opposition of stupidity, laziness, blindness and malevolence. Christ himself, of whom the Fathers of the Church say that his agony is the source of the strength of the martyrs,[13] and whose earthly life was entirely permeated and formed by his readiness for sacrificial death, to which he went "like a lamb to the slaughter"—Christ drove the money-changers from the temple with a whip; and when the most patient of men stood before the high priest and was struck in the face by a servant, he did *not* turn the other cheek, but answered: "If there was harm in what I said, tell us what was harmful in it, but if not, why dost thou strike me?" (John 18:23).

31

Thomas Aquinas, in his commentary on St. John's Gospel, has pointed to the apparent contradiction between this scene (as well as the one from the Acts of the Apostles, referred to below) and the injunction of the Sermon on the Mount: "I say unto you, resist not evil; if one strike you on the right cheek, offer him the other" (Matt. 5:39). A passivistic exegesis is quite unable to solve this "contradiction." Thomas explains (in agreement with Augustine): "Holy Scripture must be understood in the light of what Christ and the saints have actually practiced. Christ did not offer his other cheek, nor Paul either. Thus to interpret the injunction of the Sermon on the Mount *literally* is to misunderstand it. This injunction signifies rather the readiness of the soul to bear, *if it be necessary*, such things and worse, without bitterness against the attacker. This readiness our Lord showed, when he gave up his body to be crucified. That response of the Lord was useful, therefore, for our instruction."[14]

Similarly, the Apostle Paul, although his whole life was orientated toward martyrdom, did not suffer it in silence when, at the command of the high priest, he was "struck on the mouth" by the bystanders for his bold speech before the Sanhedrin; rather, he answered the high priest: "It is God that will smite thee for the whitened wall that thou art; thou art sitting there to judge me according to the law, and wilt thou break the law by ordering them to smite me?" (Acts 23:3).

The readiness to meet the supreme test by dying in patient endurance so that the good may be realized does not exclude the willingness to fight and to attack. Indeed, it is from this readiness that the springs of action in the Christian receive that detachment and freedom which, in the last analysis, are denied to every sort of tense and strained activism.

V. VITAL, MORAL, MYSTIC FORTITUDE

THE VIRTUE OF FORTITUDE keeps man from so loving his life that he loses it.

This principle—that he who loves his life loses it—is valid for every order of human reality: in the "premoral" order of mental health, in the actually "moral" order of natural ethics, in the "super-moral" order of supernatural life. In all three orders, therefore, a special significance attaches to fortitude. Only in the second order is it a "human virtue" in the strict sense; in the first it ranks below, and in the third, above it.

All three orders can be clearly separated only in the mind; in the reality of human existence they interlock. No one can say in a specific case where the sphere of moral guilt ends and the sphere of mental and psychical illness begins; and in the Christian era there is no such thing as "purely natural" virtue without actual reference to the order of grace. Thus fortitude, too, ranges through all these orders in what may be called a unified human attitude of mind and being.

To the modern science of psychology, we owe the insight that the lack of courage to accept injury and the incapability of self-sacrifice belong to the deepest sources of psychic illness. All neuroses seem to have as a common symptom an egocentric anxiety, a tense and self-centered concern for security, the inability to "let go"; in short, that kind of love for one's own life that leads straight to the loss of life. It is a very significant and by no means accidental fact that modern psychology frequently quotes the Scriptural words: "He who loves his life will lose it." Above and beyond their immediate religious significance they denote accurately the psychiatric-characterological diagnosis: that "the ego will become involved in ever greater danger the more carefully one tries to protect it."[1]

This pre-moral fortitude, as a source of psychic health closely connected with the sphere of vitality, is, in a manner beyond conscious control, linked to, and permeated by, properly moral fortitude; the moral force which, by virtue of *anima forma corporis*, works its formative effect in the sphere of the natural. On the other hand, and in a no less complicated interplay, the pre-moral fortitude seems to be the prerequisite and foundation of the essential spiritual fortitude of the man and the Christian, which grows from the soil of a fortitude rooted in the vital forces.

Christian fortitude, in the spiritual and intellectual sense, develops in proportion to the degrees of perfection proper to the interior life.

Although the supernatural ranks in essence incomparably higher than the order of nature, the former is, to begin with, less perfectly "in the possession" of man. The natural vital powers of body and mind are man's immediate and, so to speak, wholly subservient property; the supernatural life of faith, hope, and charity is only indirectly his own. Only by the unfolding of the gifts of the Holy Ghost, which are bestowed on the Christian together with the theological virtue of charity, can supernatural life become our "full possession" to such an extent that, as second nature, it urges us as though "naturally" on to sanctity.[2]

Accordingly, the degrees of perfection of Christian fortitude correspond to the degrees of unfolding of the gift of fortitude—the fortitude we owe to grace, and which belongs to the seven gifts of the Holy Ghost.

St. Thomas Aquinas distinguishes three degrees of perfection in fortitude (as in all cardinal virtues). The lowest—which on the next higher degree is not "left behind" but absorbed—is the "political" fortitude of everyday, normal community life. Almost everything that has so far been said about fortitude (excepting the references to martyrdom) applies to this—in the Christian sense— initial degree. On the road to inner progress from the first to the second and "purgatorial" purifying degree of fortitude, the man intent on a higher realization of the divine image in himself crosses the threshold of the properly mystical life. Mystical life, however, is nothing but the more perfect unfolding of the supernatural love of God and of the gifts of the Holy Spirit. The third degree of fortitude—the fortitude of the purified spirit already transformed in its essence—is attained only on the greatest heights of earthly sanctity, which are already a beginning of eternal life.[3]

Of "purgatorial fortitude," which for the average Christian represents the highest attainable degree of fortitude, Thomas says that it gives the soul the power to remain undaunted by its entrance into the higher world.[4] At first glance this seems to be a very strange proposition. But it becomes more intelligible when one considers the unanimous experience of all great mystics: at the beginning and before the final perfection of the mystic life, the soul is exposed as to a "dark night" of the senses and the spirit, in which it must think itself abandoned and lost like a man drowning on the open sea. St. John of the Cross, the mystic doctor, says that in the "dark fire" of this night—which is a true purgatory whose torment ineffably exceeds any self-imposed penance that an ascetic could imagine—God cleanses with inexorably healing hand the senses and the spirit from the dross of sin.

The Christian who dares to take the leap into this darkness and relinquishes the hold of his anxiously grasping hand, totally abandoning himself to God's absolute control, thus realizes in a very strict sense the nature of fortitude; for the sake of love's perfection he walks straight up to dreadfulness; he is not afraid to lose his life for Life's sake; he is ready to be slain by the sight of the Lord ("No man beholdeth me and liveth"—Ex. 33:20).

At this point the true significance of the expression

"heroic virtue" first becomes evident: the basis of this stage of the inner life, whose nature is the unfolding of the gifts of the Holy Spirit,[5] is in fact fortitude, the virtue which is in a very special sense, primarily and by name, an "heroic" virtue, that is, the fortitude exalted by grace, the fortitude of the mystic life. The great teacher of Christian mysticism, Teresa of Avila, says that fortitude ranks first and foremost among the prerequisites of perfection. In her autobiography we find the decisively formulated statement: "I assert that an imperfect human being needs more fortitude to pursue the way of perfection than suddenly to become a martyr."[6]

On this higher degree of fortitude, which the martyr attains, as it were, in one powerful, audacious leap, the natural forces of endurance fail. They are replaced by the Holy Spirit of fortitude, which works "in us without us" that we may overcome the darkness and reach the steep shore of light. When, in the experience of extreme anguish, the strengthening and comforting illumination of natural certainties—the metaphysical ones not excepted—wanes and changes into the half-light of uncertainty, He gives man that unshakable though veiled supernatural certainty of the final happy victory, without which, in the supernatural order, battle and injury are objectively unbearable. In the gift of fortitude the Holy Spirit pours into the soul a confidence that overcomes all fear: namely, that He will lead man to eternal life, which is the goal and purpose of all good actions, and the final deliverance from every kind of danger.[7]

This superhuman mode of fortitude is in the absolute sense "a gift." The doctors of the Church have always applied to its victories the following words of Scripture: "For they got not possession of the land by their own sword: neither did their own arm save them. But thy right hand and thy arm, and the light of thy countenance: because thou wast pleased with them" (Psalm 43).

St. Augustine and St. Thomas associate with the spiritual gift of fortitude the beatitude "Blessed are they who hunger and thirst for justice, for they shall be filled."

The supernatural gift of fortitude by no means frees the Christian from hunger and thirst for justice; it does not release him from the painful necessity of taking upon himself, in the battle for the realization of good, injury— and even, in extreme cases, death. But the doctrinal truth of ultimate "satiation," which is only "theoretically" known and possessed at the initial stages of fortitude and of the interior life in general, rises at this higher stage to an evidence so direct and compelling as to resemble the experience of sight, hearing, and touch in the natural order: so that on the deepest ground of hunger and thirst, which incidentally lose nothing of their consuming reality, the overwhelming certainty of "being filled" flashes forth in such triumphant reality that this certainty is itself "blessedness."

These three basic forms of human fortitude—the pre-moral, the properly ethical, and the mystical—all realize the same essential image: man accepts insecurity; he surrenders confidently to the governance of higher powers; he "risks" his immediate well-being; he abandons the tense, egocentric hold of a timorous anxiety. The uniformity of this attitude of mind and being, which underlies all three modes of fortitude, exists in spite of the differences that separate the sphere of mental health from those of the morally good and of the mystic life. These differences are real, and they should not be blurred. But the tendency has been too often to isolate each sphere from the others. Their inner, essential and reciprocal connections have not been sufficiently noticed. For they it is which, in the concrete reality of human existence, relate the vital and the psychical spheres to the moral and mystic ones—in a manner, however, whose complicated interactions we in all probability will never wholly grasp.

Whoever, in the vital and psychical sphere, egocentrically strains toward complete security for himself, and is incapable of daring a venturesome undertaking, will presumably also fail when to realize the good demands the suffering of injury or, worse, of death. But here we touch a sphere in which that which is essential is never wont to appear.

With this weighty reservation in mind, it may now be said that an education aiming at the development of physical courage (which ought not to be simply equated with "physical training") belongs in a specific sense to the essential foundation of moral fortitude. On the other hand, the cure of a mental illness which has over-anxiety as its root, will rarely be successful without the simultaneous moral "conversion" of the whole man. This in turn, for the eye firmly directed on concrete existence, cannot develop in an area cut off from grace, the sacraments, the mystical life.

This living connection of moral fortitude in the stricter sense with super-moral fortitude of the mystic order is of the very greatest importance. Notably departing from the classical theology of the Church, the moral teachings of the last century have separated mystical life as in essence "extraordinary" from the "ordinary" ethical sphere, and have consequently obstructed our view of the continuity in the unfolding of the supernatural life. (This continuity is most profoundly and thoroughly presented in the magnificent work of Père Garrigou-Lagrange, *Christian Perfection and Contemplation.*[8])

It is clear that political fortitude, which consists mainly in combating outward resistance in order to help justice to realization, is of a different order than "mystic" fortitude, by virtue of which the soul, for the sake of union with God, ventures into the painful darkness of "passive purification." But quite apart from the consideration that the same basic human attitude of abandonment of self is realized in both kinds of fortitude, one must not overlook the fact that the more strictly moral fortitude of the Christian reaches essentially beyond itself, into the mystic order, which, as has been said repeatedly, is nothing other than the more perfect unfolding of the supernatural life that every Christian receives in baptism. Mystic fortitude, on the other hand, reaches so effectively into the moral (and the vital-psychical) sphere, that one may say that the inmost strength of "political" fortitude derives from the hidden abandonment of man to God, from his unconditional acceptance of insecurity, which is the risk one must take in the mystical life.

Wherever a "new generation" takes up the attack against the resisting forces of evil or against a tense obsession with a security which clings to the delusion that the disharmony of the world is fundamentally curable by cautious and correct "tactics," it is above all necessary to maintain a lively and vigilant awareness that such fighting can only reach beyond sound and fury if it draws its strongest forces from the fortitude of the mystical life, which dares to submit unconditionally to the governance of God. Without a consciously preserved connection with these reserves of strength, all struggle for the good must lose its genuineness and the inner conviction of victory, and in the end can only lead to the noisy sterility of spiritual pride.

The supernatural fortitude bestowed by grace, which is a gift of the Holy Spirit, pervades and crowns all other "natural" modes of Christian fortitude. For to be brave means not only to suffer injury and death in the struggle for the realization of the good, but also to hope for victory. Without this hope, fortitude is impossible. And the higher this victory, the more certain the

hope for it, the more man risks to gain it. The supernatural gift of fortitude, the gift of the Holy Ghost, however, is nourished by the surest hope of the final and highest victory, in which all other victories, by their hidden
reference to it, are perfected—the hope of Life Eternal.

No doubt to die without hope is harder and more
fearful than dying in the hope of eternal life. But who
would be willing to accept such nonsense as this, that it
is braver to enter death without hope? Yet whoever takes
not the *end* but the *effort* as the good can hardly avoid
this nihilistic conclusion. As St. Augustine says, it is not
injury that makes the martyr, but the fact that his action
is in accordance with truth. What matters is not the ease
or the difficulty, but "the truth of things." What matters
is the reality of Eternal Life. And the "rectitude" of hope
lies in the fact that it corresponds to this reality.

On the other hand, it is hope that, in the case of
martyrdom, is put to its most revealing and unsparing
test. It is one thing to say and suppose that one lives in
hope of life eternal, and it is another thing really to hope.
What hope actually is, no one can know more profoundly
than he who must prove himself in the supreme test of
ultimate fortitude. And to no other will it be more con-
vincingly revealed that hope for eternal life is properly a
gift, and that without this gift there can be no such thing
as truly Christian fortitude.

43

TEMPERANCE

THE FOURTH CARDINAL VIRTUE

1. SELFLESS SELF-PRESERVATION

WHAT HAVE THE WORDS "temperateness" and "temperance" come to mean in today's parlance?

The meaning of "temperance" has dwindled miserably
to the crude significance of "temperateness in eating and
drinking." We may add that this term is applied chiefly,
if not exclusively, to the designation of mere quantity,
just as "intemperance" seems to indicate only excess.
Needless to say that "temperance" limited to this meaning
cannot even remotely hint at the true nature of *temperantia*, to say nothing of expressing its full content. *Temperantia* has a wider significance and a higher rank: it is
a cardinal virtue, one of the four hinges on which swings
the gate of life.

A study of the linguistic meaning of its Greek term,
sophrosyne, and of the Latin *temperantia* reveals a much
wider range of significance. The original meaning of the
Greek word embraces "directing reason" in the widest
sense. And the Latin stays close to this far-ranging significance. In St. Paul's First Epistle to the Corinthians
(12:24f.) we read: *Deus temperavit corpus.* "Thus God
has established a harmony in the body, giving special

honor to that which needed it most. There was to be no want of unity in the body; all the different parts of it were to make each other's welfare their common care." The primary and essential meaning of *temperare*, therefore, is this: to dispose various parts into one unified and ordered whole.

Aquinas says that the second meaning of temperance is "serenity of the spirit" (*quies animi*).[1] It is obvious that this proposition does not imply a purely subjective state of mental calm or the tranquil satisfaction which is the by-product of an unassuming, leisurely life in a narrow circle. Nor does it mean a mere absence of irritation, nor dispassionate equanimity. All this need not go deeper than the surface of the intellectual and spiritual life. What is meant is the serenity that fills the inmost recesses of the human being, and is the seal and fruit of order. The purpose and goal of *temperantia* is man's inner order, from which alone this "serenity of spirit" can flow forth. "Temperance" signifies the realizing of this order within oneself.

Temperantia is distinguished from the other cardinal virtues by the fact that it refers exclusively to the active man himself. Prudence looks to all existent reality; justice to the fellow-man; the man of fortitude relinquishes, in self-forgetfulness, his own possessions and his life. Temperance, on the other hand, aims at each man himself.[2] Temperance implies that man should look to himself and his condition, that his vision and his will should be focussed on himself. That notion that the primordial images of all things reside in God has been applied by Aquinas to the cardinal virtues also: the primordial divine mode of *temperantia*, he states, is the "turning of the Divine Spirit to Itself."[3]

For man there are two modes of this turning toward the self: a selfless and a selfish one. Only the former makes for self-preservation; the latter is destructive. In modern psychology we find this thought: genuine self-preservation is the turning of man toward himself, with the essential stipulation, however, that in this movement he does not become fixed upon himself. ("Whoever fixes his eyes upon himself gives no light.") Temperance is selfless self-preservation. Intemperance is self-destruction through the selfish degradation of the powers which aim at self-preservation.

It is a commonplace though nonetheless mysterious truth that man's inner order—unlike that of the crystal, the flower, or the animal—is not a simply given and self-evident reality, but rather that the same forces from which human existence derives its being can upset that inner order to the point of destroying the spiritual and moral person. That this cleavage in human nature (provided we do not try to persuade ourselves that it does not exist) finds its explanation only in the acceptance by faith of the revealed truth of original sin, is too vast a subject to be discussed here. It seems necessary, however, to consider more closely the structure of that inner order and disorder.

Most difficult to grasp is the fact that it is indeed the essential human self that is capable of throwing itself into disorder to the point of self-destruction. For man is not really a battlefield of conflicting forces and impulses which conquer one another; and if we say that the sensuality "in us" gets the better of our reason, this is only a vague and metaphorical manner of speaking. Rather it is always our single self that is chaste or unchaste, temperate or intemperate, self-preserving or self-destructive. It is always the decisive center of the whole, indivisible person by which the inner order is upheld or upset. "It is not the good my will preserves, but the evil my will disapproves, that *I* find myself doing" (Rom. 7:19).

Also, the very powers of the human being which most readily appear as the essential powers of self-preservation, self-assertion, and self-fulfillment are at the same time the first to work the opposite: the self-destruction of the moral person. In the *Summa Theologica* we find the almost uncanny formulation: the powers whose ordering is the function of temperance "can most easily bring unrest to the spirit, because they belong to the *essence* of man."[4]

But how can it be that the very powers of self-preservation are so close to becoming destructive? How can it be that the man who seeks himself can miss himself in his very seeking? And how, on the other hand, can self-love be selfless?

A narrow gap of understanding is wedged open by a proposition of St. Thomas, which may confidently be called the basis of a metaphysical philosophy of active man. It states that to love God more than himself is in accordance with the natural being of man, as of every creature, and with his will as well.[5] Consequently, the offense against the love of God derives its self-destructive sharpness from the fact that it is likewise in conflict with the nature and the natural will of man himself. If he loves nothing so much as himself, man misses and perverts, with inner necessity, the purpose inherent in self-love as in all love: to preserve, to make real, to fulfill. This purpose is given only to selfless self-love, which seeks not itself blindly, but with open eyes endeavors to correspond to the true reality of God, the self, and the world.

The force of this metaphysical truth formulated by Aquinas strikes so deep that, in a sense, it becomes even nonsensical to desire the preservation of the inner order for its own sake and consequently to will even genuine self-preservation as such. (That the *temperantia* of the miser, who shuns debauchery because of its expense, is, as Aquinas says, no virtue, need hardly be mentioned.[6]) It is known how little, for example, a medical directive alone can do to establish true inner discipline; not unjustly has it been said of psychotherapy unrelated to either religion or metaphysics that it tends to produce an "anxiously fostered middle-class tranquillity, poisoned by its triteness,"[7] a result which evidently has nothing to do with the essential serenity of genuine temperance. This failure is no accident, but rather an inevitable consequence. The discipline of temperance cannot be realized with a view to man alone.

51

The discipline of temperance, understood as selfless self-preservation, is the preserving and defending realization of the inner order of man. For temperance not only preserves, it also defends: indeed, it preserves by defending. For since the first sin man has been not only capable of loving himself more than he loves God his Creator but, contrary to his own nature, inclined to do so. The discipline of temperance defends him against all selfish perversion of the inner order, through which alone the moral person exists and lives effectively.

Wherever forces of self-preservation, self-assertion, self-fulfillment, destroy the structure of man's inner being, the discipline of temperance and the license of intemperance enter into play.

The natural urge towards sensual enjoyment, manifested in delight in food and drink and sexual pleasure, is the echo and mirror of man's strongest natural forces of self-preservation. The basic forms of enjoyment correspond to these most primordial forces of being, which tend to preserve the individual man as well as the whole race in the existence for which they were created (Wisdom 1:14). But for the very reason that these forces are closely allied to the deepest human urge towards being, they exceed all other powers of mankind in their destructive violence once they degenerate into selfishness. Therefore, we find here the actual province of *temperantia:* temperateness and chastity, intemperateness and unchastity, are the primordial forms of the discipline of temperance and the license of intemperance[8] (see chapters II, III).

But we have not, as yet, fully explored the range of the concept of *temperantia*.—In "humility," the instinctive urge to self-assertion can also be made serviceable to genuine self-preservation, but it can likewise pervert and miss this purpose in "pride"[9] (ch. vi).—And if the natural desire of man to avenge an injustice which he has suffered and to restore his rights explodes in uncontrollable fury, it destroys that which can only be preserved by "gentleness" and "mildness"[10] (ch. vii). Without rational self-restraint even the natural hunger for sense-perception or for knowledge can degenerate into a destructive and pathological compulsive greed; this degradation Aquinas calls *curiositas*, the disciplined mode *studiositas*[11] (ch. viii).

To sum up: chastity, continence, humility, gentleness, mildness, *studiositas*, are modes of realization of the discipline of temperance; unchastity, incontinence, pride, uninhibited wrath, *curiositas*, are forms of intemperance.

II. CHASTITY AND UNCHASTITY

In CURRENT TREATISES on chastity and unchastity, the air one breathes is not always bracing.

This state of affairs may have various causes, one of which is certainly this: in contradiction to the true grading and order of things, the realm of sex—again for many different reasons—has moved to the center of attention for the general moral consciousness. In addition to this, and despite all contrary statements of principle, a smoldering subterranean Manichaeism casts suspicion on everything pertaining to physical reproduction as being somehow impure, defiling, and beneath the true dignity of man. From all these and other hidden discords are brewed the oppressive mists of casuistry and distortion, of embarrassment and importunity, which frequently pervade discussions of chastity and unchastity.

On the other hand, it is a refreshing and emancipating experience to read the tractate on the same subject by Aquinas, in his *Summa Theologica*, written with truly holy candor and concise cleanness. Then we realize with joy that we have the right (and more than the right!) to adhere to the principles taught by this "Universal Doctor" of the Church.

To begin with: for Thomas it is plainly self-evident —indeed so self-evident that it need hardly be mentioned even to those but moderately instructed—(while it may still be well not to remain silent on this point)—that the sexual powers are not necessarily an evil but really a good. With Aristotle he says incisively that there is something divine in human seed.[1] It is equally self-evident to Thomas's thinking that, "like eating and drinking," the fulfillment of the natural sexual urge and its accompanying pleasure are good and not in the least sinful, assuming, of course, that order and moderation are preserved.[2] For the intrinsic purpose of sexual power, namely, that not only now but also in days to come the children of man may dwell upon the earth and in the Kingdom of God, is not merely a good, but, as Thomas says, "a surpassing good."[3] Indeed, complete asensuality, unfeelingly averse to all sexual pleasure, which some would fain regard as "properly" perfect and ideal according to Christian doctrine, is described in the *Summa Theologica* not only as an imperfection but actually as a moral defect (*vitium*).[4]

At this point, a deliberate digression is forthwith called for. The progenitive purpose of sexuality is not the sole and exclusive purpose of marriage. Yet marriage is the proper fulfillment of sexual power. Of the three goods of marriage: community of life, offspring, and sacramental blessing (*fides, proles, sacramentum*), it is the mutually benevolent and inviolable community of life which, according to Aquinas, is the special benefit conferred on man "as man."[5]

This affirmative position is clear to Thomas beyond any doubt because, more perhaps than any other Christian teacher, he takes seriously the fundamental thought of revelation: "Everything created by God is good" and thinks it through to its conclusion. These words were used by the Apostle Paul in order to reprimand, with the same reference to creation, those "hypocritical liars" who carry a "torch in their conscience" and "forbid men to marry and to enjoy certain foods" (I Timothy 4:2f.). Heresy and hyperasceticism are and always have been close neighbors. The Father of the Church, St. John Chrysostom, has expressed this with great emphasis; in a sermon he links the words of Scripture concerning "two in one flesh" to the physical union of the spouses and adds: "Why do you blush? Is it not pure? You are behaving like heretics!"[6]

"The more necessary something is, the more the order of reason must be preserved in it."[7] For the very reason that sexual power is so noble and necessary a good, it needs the preserving and defending order of reason.

Chastity as a virtue, therefore, is constituted in its essence by this and nothing else, namely that it realizes the order of reason in the province of sexuality.[8] Unchastity as a sin, on the other hand, is in its essence the transgression and violation of the rational order in the province of sexuality.[9]

There is something uncomfortable about the straightforward use of the terms "reason" and "the order of reason" for us modern Christians. But this mistrust, for which, by the way, there is ample cause and reason, must not prevent us from a frank inquiry into what Thomas would have us understand by "reason" and "the order of reason."

Four facts have to be borne in mind if we wish to escape the danger of simply missing St. Thomas's meaning, even before taking a position ourselves. We must consider that Thomas's concept of "reason" and "the order of reason" is to be taken realistically, not idealistically; that it is free of all rationalistic restrictions; that it has none of the connotations of the *ratio* of the Enlightenment; and, finally, that it is not in the least spiritualistic.

The concept "order of reason," first of all, does not signify that something must agree with the imperative of an "absolute reason" detached from its object. *Reason* includes a reference to reality; indeed, it is itself this reference. "In accord with reason" is in this sense that which is right "in itself," that which corresponds to reality itself.[10] The order of reason accordingly signifies that something is disposed in accordance with the truth of real things.

Secondly: *Ratio* is not that reason which arbitrarily restricts itself to the province of purely natural cognition. *Ratio* here signifies—in its widest sense—man's power to grasp reality. Now, man grasps reality not only in natural cognition but also—and this reality is a higher object of knowledge and the process of grasping it a higher process—by faith in the revelation of God. If therefore the *Summa Theologica* states that Christ is the chief Lord (*principalis Dominus*), the first owner of our bodies, and that one who uses his body in a manner contrary to order, injures Christ the Lord Himself,[11] Thomas is not of the opinion that this proposition exceeds[12] the pattern of "mere" rational order, but rather that for Christian thought to be guided by divine revelation is the very highest form of "accord with reason"—this in spite of the fact that elsewhere Thomas knows how to distinguish sharply between natural and supernatural cognition. "The order of reason," accordingly, is the order which corresponds to the reality made evident to man through faith and knowledge.

Thirdly, the emphatic and ever recurrent stress on reason and the order of reason in the works of Aquinas is obviously not to be understood in the sense which the Enlightenment has given to these terms. "To realize the order of reason in the province of sexuality" is a proposition which one most certainly would not want to understand as an incitement or permission to lift that which natural feeling and propriety surround and protect with the sheltering obscurity of concealment and silence into the crude and artificial light of a shallow "know-it-all" view. Rather, Thomas expressly coordinates modesty with chastity, whose function is to see to it that this silence and this obscurity are not destroyed either by shamelessness or uninhibited rationalizing, or spotlighted by the methods of "sexual instruction."[13] This, therefore, forms part of the "order of reason" too.

Fourthly, the Thomistic concept of reason might be misinterpreted spiritualistically, a facile temptation to some. The proposition that "the essential and proper good of man is existence in accord with reason"[14] could be read to mean: "Constant spiritual awareness is what distinguishes the specifically human condition; everything that clouds this awareness is unspiritual, consequently unworthy of the human condition, and therefore evil." Applied to the province here under discussion such a spiritualistic interpretation might easily lead to the following conclusion: "In the act of procreation, reason is so overwhelmed by the abundance of pleasure that, as the philosopher says, spiritual cognition becomes impossible . . .; thus there can be no act of begetting without sin." Now this last sentence is actually to be found in the *Summa Theologica* of St. Thomas—but as an "objection," that is, as an expressly confuted opinion, as a negation to which a clear affirmation is opposed. The affirmation is worded as follows: "As long as the sexual act itself corresponds to the rational order, the abundance of pleasure does not conflict with the proper mean of virtue. . . . And even the fact that reason is unable to make a free act of cognition of spiritual things simultaneously with that pleasure does not prove that the sexual act conflicts with virtue. For it is not against virtue that the workings of reason sometimes are interrupted by something that takes place in accordance with reason: otherwise it would be contrary to virtue to sleep."[15] Do we need any further explanation in order to show how much St. Thomas's concept of reason has regard to the *whole* man—to body and soul, sensuality and spirituality? St. Thomas designates as "not in accord with reason" the opinion of some Fathers of the Church that "in Paradise the propagation of mankind would have taken place in some other manner, such as that of the angels";[16] indeed, St. Thomas says: the pleasure that accompanies intercourse must have been even stronger in Paradise—since mental awareness was unclouded and because of the greater delicacy of human nature and the higher sensitivity of the body.[17] But enough of this.

Only on the basis of these four delimitations and refutations is our vision liberated so that we can see the true core of the proposition that chastity, by disciplining sexuality, realizes the order of reason.

The order of reason, however, implies, first, that the immanent purpose of sexual power be not perverted but fulfilled (in marriage, with its threefold "good"); second, that the inner structure of the moral person be kept intact; and, third, that justice between men be not infringed. What we are concerned with here is the purpose of sex as it was intended originally in the first creation, and ennobled by Christ in the New Creation; what we are concerned with is the existential structure of the moral person, as established in nature and in grace; what we are concerned with is order among men as guaranteed not merely by natural justice, but also by the higher justice of *caritas*, that is, supernatural love of God and man.

Chastity realizes in the province of sex the order which corresponds to the truth of the world and of man both as experienced and as revealed, and which accords with the twofold form of this truth—not that of unveiled evidence alone, but that of veiled evidence also—that is, of mystery.

It is not adultery only which touches upon the provinces of both *temperantia* and justice;[18] rather, any unchastity has these two aspects: to be at once intemperance and injustice. St. Thomas relates the totality of all sins against chastity to the "common weal"—taking this term in a very profound and far-reaching sense—and to justice as well;[19] similarly he relates all the ten commandments, not excepting the sixth and the ninth, to justice.[20] For example, the *Summa Theologica* says of "*simplex fornicatio*," that is, sexual intercourse of unmarried persons, in which neither the right of a spouse, as in adultery, nor the liberty of the person, as in rape, is violated: "Any sin is mortal that is a direct attempt upon a human life. *Fornicatio simplex* involves a disorder that results in injury to the life of a human being, namely, the child to be born from such intercourse. *Simplex fornicatio* is contrary to the welfare of the child to be reared, and *for this reason it is a mortal sin.*"[21]

We have become used to see in adultery, and even more in adulterous desire and cupidity, as in sexual transgressions generally, almost exclusively the element of lust, neglecting almost completely the element of injustice. Yet it is very important that the collective moral consciousness of Christianity should again assign greater weight to this objective side of chastity which is concerned with the common weal and with justice, as against a view limited exclusively to the subjective factor. To restore the proper emphasis is evidently important not only because it corresponds to actual fact and truth, but also because the neglect or insufficient observation of the objective element of justice in chastity and its opposite derives from an erroneous conception of man and at the same time causes and perpetuates this error.

In this book, which treats of *temperantia* and not of the sixth commandment nor of marriage nor of the Christian idea of man as a whole, nor of justice, it is quite enough that this thought has been given emphatic expression.

Here, however, it is our purpose to consider chastity and unchastity expressly from the point of view of moderation and its opposite, being fully aware, at the same time, of the limitations inherent in the subject. We shall speak first not of its outward repercussions, but of its root in the inner man: of the disciplining of the sex urge by the spiritual directing power of reason, and also of the abdication of the spirit, which opens the way for sex to destroy the moral person.

In what way and why does unchastity destroy the structure of the person?

Unchastity most effectively falsifies and corrupts the

virtue of prudence.[22] All that conflicts with the virtue of prudence stems for the most part from unchastity;[23] unchastity begets a blindness of spirit which practically excludes all understanding of the goods of the spirit;[24] unchastity splits the power of decision;[25] on the contrary, the virtue of chastity more than any other makes man capable and ready for contemplation.[26]

All these propositions of St. Thomas do not refer to isolated effects and consequences; if the spirit is blinded by unchastity, it is not by a process similar to the wilting of a plant in a rainless period. This blindness is of the essence of unchastity itself, which is by its very nature destructive. It is not its outward effect and consequence, but its immanent essential property.

"The being of man in its essential significance consists in this: to be in accord with reason. If therefore a man keeps to what is in accord with reason, he is said 'to keep himself in himself.' "[27] Unchastity destroys in a very special manner this self-possession and this human "keeping of oneself in oneself." Unchaste abandon and the self-surrender of the soul to the world of sensuality paralyzes the primordial powers of the moral person: the ability to perceive, in silence, the call of reality, and to make, in the retreat of this silence, the decision appropriate to the concrete situation of concrete action. This is the meaning inherent in all those propositions which speak of the falsification and corruption of prudence, of the blindness of the spirit, and of the splitting of the power of decision.

Now all this is not to be understood as if the corruptive effect of unchastity derived from the fact that the spirit turns to the "sensual" and "inferior" in general. On the contrary, such turning is altogether inevitable for any decision. It is indeed of the essence of the virtue of prudence that it face squarely all those concrete realities which surround man's concrete actions. Accordingly, it is not the reference to the province of sexuality that produces the blindness and deafness brought about by unchastity; such an opinion would be Manichaean at bottom, and therefore anti-Christian.

Rather, the destructiveness lies in the fact that unchastity constricts man and thus renders him incapable of seeing objective reality. An unchaste man wants above all something for himself; he is distracted by an unobjective "interest"; his constantly strained will-to-pleasure prevents him from confronting reality with that selfless detachment which alone makes genuine knowledge possible. St. Thomas here uses the comparison with a lion who, at the sight of a stag, is unable to perceive anything but the anticipated meal. In an unchaste heart, attention is not merely fixed upon a certain track, but the "window" of the soul has lost its "transparency," that is, its capacity for perceiving existence, as if a selfish interest had covered it, as it were, with a film of dust. (We cannot repeat too often: only he who is silent hears, only the invisible is transparent.)

This kind of interestedness is altogether selfish. The abandonment of an unchaste heart to the sensual world has nothing in common with the genuine dedication of a

64

searcher for truth to the reality of being, of a lover to his beloved. Unchastity does not dedicate itself, it offers itself. It is selfishly intent upon the "prize," upon the reward of illicit lust. "Chaste," says St. Augustine, "is the heart that loves God without looking for reward."[28] One further comment! For anyone whose function it is to lead and counsel young people, it is extremely important to keep in mind and to make known that it is this selfishness which characterizes the inner nature of unchastity (as intemperance). Where the selfish motive is absent, we may speak of thoughtlessness, curiosity, or of impulses so completely natural that they lie outside the scope of moral judgment—but not of unchastity.

This perversion of a genuine process of knowing is all the more destructive the more immediately a given knowledge concerns man himself and the more it can be the foundation of moral decisions.[29] Not only is the cognitive process thereby poisoned and perverted, but also the power of decision itself, and even more so; "most of all prudence," says Aquinas.[30] It is prudence, however, which, as the perfection of conscience, is the innermost source-region of the moral person. Prudence implies a transformation of the knowledge of truth into decisions corresponding to reality. This transformation is achieved in three steps: deliberation, judgment, decision.[31] Upon each of these three steps the destructive power of intemperance manifests itself: in place of deliberation guided by the truth of things, we find complete recklessness and inconsideration; a hasty judgment that will not wait until reason has weighed the pros and cons; and even if a correct decision were reached, it would always be endangered by the fickleness of a heart that abandons itself indiscriminately to the surging mass of sensual impressions.[32] This is inevitable: if you do not move a knife in the plane of the thing to be cut, it cannot cut at all. So without a direct, innocent, and selfless vision of reality there can be no interior order of the moral person and no honest moral decision.

Chastity, on the other hand, renders one able to and ready not only for the perception of reality and thus also for decision corresponding to reality, but also for that highest mode of relating oneself to reality in which the purest dedication to knowledge and the most selfless dedication in love become one, namely, contemplation, in which man turns toward the divine Being and becomes aware of that truth which is at once the highest good.

To be open to the truth of real things and to live by the truth that one has grasped is the essence of the moral being. Only when we recognize this state of things can we likewise understand the depths to which the unchaste heart permits destruction to invade its very being.

This dark portrayal of the destructive force of unchastity applies in all its harshness only to unchastity as *intemperantia*, but not to unchastity as *incontinentia*; just as that which has been said of chastity is fully pertinent only to chastity as *temperantia* but not to chastity as *continen-*

tia.[33] This significant distinction must be briefly explained.

Because it *is* not always the same thing when two people *do* the same thing, a moral doctrine which regards only the actions of man but not his being, is always in danger of seeing only the sameness (or the difference) of the actions, and missing important differences (or samenesses) at a greater depth. Since, however, the moral theology of the Universal Doctor of the Church is a doctrine of virtue—that is: a doctrine of the *being* of man as the source of his actions—the difference between *temperantia-intemperantia* on the one hand and *continentia-incontinentia* on the other hand could not easily escape him.

Chastity as *temperantia*, or unchastity as *intemperantia!* This means that each, respectively, has become a deep-rooted basic attitude of man, and, as it were, a second nature to him. Chastity as *continentia*, or unchastity as *incontinentia!* This means that neither is necessarily based on what might be called a natural inclination of being; neither has as yet grown firm roots in the existential core of man. This second mode of chastity is not the perfected virtue of temperance and moderation, but a strenuous control; and this mode of unchastity is not a consummate intemperance, but a mere lack of control. Chastity as control is only a tentative sketch; chastity as *temperantia* is perfected realization. The first is less perfect than the second, because by the former, the directing power of reason has only been able to mold the conscious will, but not yet the sensual urge, whereas by the latter will

67

and urge are both stamped with "rational order."[34] In Thomas's explicit opinion, the effort of self-control pertains only to the less perfect steps of the beginner, whereas real, perfected virtue, by the very nature of its concept, bears the joyous, radiant seal of ease, of effortlessness, of self-evident inclination.[35] On the other hand, unchastity in the form of lack of self-control is less pernicious, less sinful, than unchastity in the form of actual intemperance. In the first case, as Aristotle[36] and St. Thomas[37] say, the best is not lost; the principle, the ground of being, subsists, namely, the right conception of the direction of will toward the true goal; and through this unblemished rightness even the sensual urge can be reintegrated again and again into its order: he who sins from lack of control is quick to repent;[38] and repentance is the repudiation of sin. On the other hand, he who sins from a deep-rooted basic attitude of intemperance directs his will expressly toward sin; he does not repent easily; indeed, "he is happy to have sinned, because sinning has become 'natural' for him."[39] The merely uncontrolled can be "recalled" to order; actual intemperance, however, is not easily revocable.[40] To sin from a basic attitude of one's will is real malice; to sin in a gust of passion is weakness—*infirmitas*.[41] One who is merely uncontrolled *is* not unchaste, even though he *acts* unchastely.[42]

It is no doubt easy to see that to stress this difference is not to indulge in the pleasure of theoretical hair-splitting. Rather, it is an effort to establish a contrast which acquires an immediately practical significance, both pedagogical and pastoral.

It is *temperantia*, the virtue that realizes the inner order of man in himself which St. Thomas has in mind when—in contrast to justice, in whose province that which is "properly and in itself right" can and must be determined—speaking of "the other moral virtues which refer to the passions and in which right or wrong cannot be determined in the same fashion, because men vary in their attitudes toward the passions," he says, "therefore it is necessary that what is right and reasonable in the passions should be determined with reference to *ourselves*, who are moved by the passions."[43] But especially in the province of *temperantia* "we ourselves" have the choice of innumerable possibilities: e.g., to desire half-heartedly or whole-heartedly, to tolerate, to let things take their course, to give in to pressure or to be carried away. "Who could determine," writes the perceptive Thomist, H. D. Noble, in his commentary on the French edition of Aquinas[44]—"who could determine when lack of control ends and when actual intemperance begins?"

St. Thomas says that the realization of *temperantia* varies too much according to individuals and periods to allow the establishment of hard and fast, universally valid commandments on *temperantia*.[45] The whole realm of "unchaste thoughts, desires, words, looks, etc." which in the casuistic manuals occupies so much space, is treated in the *Summa Theologica* in a single article of not quite one page in length. It determines the general principle only, that not the accomplished sinful act alone is sinful, but also the willing consent to the pleasure imagined and implicit in this act; for this willing consent is inconceivable without an attitude of acceptance towards the accomplished act itself;[46] everything, therefore, which derives from such willing consent is likewise a sin.[47]

Within this frame of reference it should certainly be possible to construe, after the manner of the casuist, a series of typical "individual cases" exemplifying the springs of action, a simplified and meaningful "scheme" of human behavior. But how are we to react to a proposition such as this one, found in one of the most popular handbooks of moral theology: "To look at the private parts of animals out of curiosity, but without voluptuousness . . . is a venial sin"? Not to mention other distortions,[48] it seems that here the limit beyond which casuistry becomes meaningless has been considerably exceeded. Propositions so constructed seem entirely to miss the true purpose and scope of casuistry which is to provide a tentative approach and an auxiliary means for the practice of discernment. Is it not to be feared that a discernment schooled by such methods will be misguided toward an unrealistic rigidity and a prematurely fixed judgment, instead of towards a sober evaluation of the realities of life; and that this in turn may lead to a total incomprehension of the reality of man as a being who responds to the richly orchestrated world with every power of his soul, and thus reaches his choice?

We have spoken of the destructive power of unchastity and of the preserving, perfecting, fulfilling power of chastity. Something more must be added to this subject.

Without chastity, not only is the satiation of the spirit with truth rendered impossible, but also actual sensual joy in what is sensually beautiful. That Christian doctrine does not exclude sensual enjoyment from the realm of the morally good (as against the merely "permissible") does not need to be specifically stated. But that this enjoyment should be made possible only by the virtue of temperance and moderation—that, indeed, is a surprising thought. Yet this is what we read in the *Summa Theologica*, in the first question of the tractate on temperance[49]—even if more between and behind the lines than in what is said directly. In the case of animals, it is said there, no pleasure is derived from the activity of the other senses, such as the eye and the ear, except as they affect the satisfaction of the drives of hunger and sex; only because of the promise of food is the lion "happy" when he spies a stag or hears his call. Man, by contrast, is able to enjoy what is seen or heard for the sensual "appropriateness" alone which appeals to the eye and the ear—by this, nothing else but sensual beauty is to be understood.[50] One frequently reads and hears that in intemperance man sinks to the level of the beast—a sentence to be used with caution, for intemperance (like temperance) is something exclusively human; neither angel nor animal can know it. But keeping this distinction in mind the sentence becomes meaningful: unchaste lust has the tendency to relate the whole complex of the sensual world, and particularly of sensual beauty, to sexual pleasure exclusively. Therefore only a chaste sensuality can realize the specifically human faculty of perceiving sensual beauty, such as that of the human body, as beauty, and to enjoy it for its own sake, for its "sensual appropriateness," undeterred and unsullied by the self-centered will to pleasure. It has been said that only the pure of heart can laugh freely and liberatingly. It is no less true that only those who look at the world with pure eyes can experience its beauty.

Unlike all other virtues, it has always been the strange fate of the virtue of temperance and moderation, especially in its aspect of chastity, not to be valued and practiced or scorned and ridiculed more or less at its face value, but to be overestimated and overvalued in a very specific sense. This is something altogether unique. There have, of course, always been theoretical discussions about the hierarchy of the virtues, and one or the other has been shifted to a higher rank. But the stubborn and really quite fanatical preference given to *temperantia*, especially to chastity, which runs through the whole history of Christian doctrine as a more or less hidden undercurrent or countercurrent, has a very special aspect. No one, at any rate, has attached to justice or prudence or to any of the three theological virtues such an emphatic and evidently not simply factual, but emotionally charged, evaluation.

Of course, there would not be the slightest objection against such an evaluation *per se*—for strictly speaking, virtues as such cannot be overrated. But here we are speaking of an evaluation and overevaluation based on a false premise; of an evaluation, therefore, which implies a misunderstanding of what is supposedly valued so highly. And against this we must object strongly.

72

In the province of *temperantia*, as we have said before, it is man's attitude toward creation which is decided, and most incisively. And the "wrong premise" upon which rest the overevaluation and erroneous value given to *temperantia* in general and chastity in particular amounts to this, namely the explicit or implied opinion that the sensual reality of the whole of creation, and above all the non-spiritual element in man himself, is actually evil. To sum up: the "wrong premise" is an explicit, or, more often, an implicit, even unconscious and unintended, Manichaeism.

That man must eat, that he must sleep, that the origin of new human life is linked to the physical union of man and woman—all this, especially the last, appears, in this presumably ineradicable apprehension of the world, as a necessary evil—perhaps not even a necessary one—something unworthy of God the Creator and of man as well. The specifically human task, or better still, the specifically Christian task, would consist in rising above this entire "lower" sphere and mounting by ascetic practice to a purely spiritual way of life. Not only do fasting, vigils, and sexual continence take on a very special importance from this basic approach, but they move necessarily into the center of attention of the man striving for perfection. This evaluation, however, shares and indeed intensifies the errors of its origin; and despite all outward similarity, it has as little to do with the Christian evaluation of those three things as the heresies of the Manichees, the Montanists, and the Cathari have to do with the Catholic dogma that proclaims that created reality is good in all its spheres, and is not subject to the arbitrariness of human evaluation; indeed, it is the basis and the point of departure of all evaluation as well as of all realization of value.[51]

That "wrong premise" and its effects on ethical doctrine is particularly evident in the Montanist writings of Tertullian, who, by reason of his ambiguous status as a quasi-Father of the Church (St. Thomas speaks of him only as an heretic: *haereticus, Tertullianus nomine*)[52] has continued to this day as the ancestor and the chief witness of that erroneous evaluation of *temperantia*. One need only enumerate the subjects of his works: "On Modesty," "On the Veiling of Virgins," "On the Adornment of Women," "On Fasting," "Admonition to Chastity," "Concerning Stage Plays," or mention his rejection of second marriages after the death of wife or husband, in order to show that the realm of *temperantia* is very prominently under scrutiny. For Tertullian, unchastity is to such a point the primal form of sin that according to him the sin of the angels was unchastity, and thus they fell from God; this is what he thought St. Paul had in mind when he said that women should veil themselves "because of the angels" (I Cor. 4:10).[53] To the same frame of reference belongs the cause of Tertullian's separation from the Church only a few years after his baptism: he could neither comprehend nor condone the fact that Pope Callistus welcomed back into the ecclesiastical community those sinners against chastity who had done the required penance contritely. Tertullian denounces the encyclical with which the Pope proclaims this measure as a blot upon the Church, fit to be read "in those dens of vice, beneath the signboards of the whorehouses rather than in the house of God."[54] It is characteristic, also, that already with Tertullian the emphasis on external action appears which customarily and as if from inner necessity accompanies the erroneous evaluation of *temperantia*, and more especially of chastity: he calls for more obligatory fast days; for the veiling of women and girls; and he sees the hallmark of a Christian in his abstention from public entertainments.[55]

Blindness only can deny that this Manichaean undervaluation of the sensual reality of creation (let us repeat: not as a formulated opinion, but as an inarticulate attitude) tinges and surreptitiously qualifies the current Christian notion of the virtue of temperance, and more especially of chastity. This becomes evident in innumerable small traits pertaining to the thinking and speaking habits of Christian folk, and also not infrequently in the accents and shadings of moral preaching itself.

If, for example, one speaks with special emphasis of the defilement of unchastity, this implies a different and weightier blame than the defilement pertaining to any other sin. (Actually, the term "defilement" is almost never applied to other sins.) What is censured is not only the specific "vulgarity" inherent in any form of self-indulging pleasure; there is also almost always a persistently audible undertone suggesting the idea of contact with something in itself impure, with a reality defiling *per se*.

75

The current notion of the "Immaculate Conception" —current even among Christians—refers this immaculateness not so much to the person of the Virgin Mary as rather to the process of conception, *e.g.*, of begetting (and often enough, as anyone can test, not to the conception of Mary, but to that of the Lord in the womb of his mother). Among people generally, this immaculateness is in any case not understood as it is understood by the Church and by theology, namely as signifying that Mary was free from the stain of original sin from her mother's womb. The current popular notion, rather, is this: by a special grace of God, that conception remained free from the impurity and taint which naturally adheres to it, as to all begetting and conception. And even if this immaculateness is correctly referred to the person of the Virgin Mary herself, as in the appellation Mary "Immaculate," we find on close listening that the concept has been totally deprived of its universal, inclusive significance, and has been limited to the province of chastity alone.—Something similar is true of the concept of purity, which, also viewed Biblically, is much broader in scope than chastity. For the average understanding it has become entirely natural to refer the beatitude "Blessed are the pure in heart" exclusively, or at any rate principally, to chastity, though neither the immediate Biblical meaning nor the interpretation of these words of the Lord in classical theology favors such restriction; Aquinas, for example, by no means assigns the beatitude of the pure in heart to the virtue of chastity, but to the supernatural virtue of faith.[56]—Finally: Try to ascertain what the aver-

76

age Christian associates with the sentence: To the pure all things are pure. First, he will not readily imagine that this phrase is to be found in the New Testament (Titus 1:15) and that it only affirms what was said by Jesus himself (Matt. 15:10-20); on the contrary, the average Christian, such as we find him in every walk of life and on every educational level, would sooner have guessed at a non-Christian, liberal author. And it is scarcely ever thought of that aside from and indeed predating its misused liberal interpretation, this sentence has a sound and important Christian significance. Of course here again purity is confined to chastity, in evident contradiction to the sense of the context.[57] And since the presumably Christian sense of the Biblical sentence is supposed to imply that even to the pure man *not* everything is pure, we find here again the effects of the notion of the essential impurity of the reality of being.

These misconceptions, which miss the actual Christian meaning of things—and examples of which could be multiplied—can only be partially attributed to ignorance. They propagate themselves, in the form of inarticulate opinions and attitudes, beneath and beyond and even in spite of formal instruction; as a rule, the average Christian we here have in mind will, after some concentration on the relevant article in his catechism, be able to give the "theoretically" correct answer. Decisive, however, are not so much the explicit words as the atmosphere in the province of moral education and teaching; and it must be admitted by even the most cautious judgment that this atmosphere is plainly not entirely free from the germs of Manichaeism. And no cleansing can be effected by mere theoretical knowledge and cognition, or by instruction only. What is required is that the dogmatic truth of God the Creator and His works be wholly appropriated in humbly confident assent, and that this truth obtain the radiant and vivifying power which is the exclusive property of genuine vitality.

But the "world" exists not only as God's creation. There is also the "world" which, as St. John the Apostle says, "lies in evil" and prevails in the "gratification of corrupt nature, gratification of the eyes, and the empty pomp of living" (I John 22:16); there is the kingdom of the "Prince of this world" (John 12:31, Luke 4:6); there is the world for which Christ the Lord did not want to pray (John 17:9). There is not only the reality of creation, but also the perversion of the order of creation, which has taken on form in the activities of men and the objective "creations" which grow out of these. And this "world" also comes up for judgment in the sphere of *temperantia*, in a very specific sense. It is in that which aids and abets the self-indulging lust for pleasure that the inversion of the order of creation may most obtrusively be realized, filling the foreground of the "world" completely with its seductive call. (Though of course the core and substance of that world which lies in evil consists primarily in the realization of injustice and above all in the actual denial of faith, hope, and charity—a telling counterpart to the hierarchy of the virtues!) From this point of view the evaluation and the educational emphasis put on the virtue of temperance rightly achieves special significance. This sort of estimate of *temperantia*, however, has to be carefully distinguished from the previously mentioned "Manichaean" variety (not always an easy task, as the Manichaeans constantly adduce the valid arguments of the other side together with their own). Even the rigorist attitude of the Carthaginian Tertullian is partially conditioned by his constant experience of metropolitan life. "It is bad to live in cities: there are too many lecherous people," reads the beginning of the chapter on chastity in Nietzsche's *Zarathustra*. What Nietzsche asserts with hard-hitting precision was also known to Thomas, who formulates it more dispassionately and abstractly: "There is not much sinning because of natural desires. . . . But the stimuli of desire which man's cunning has devised are something else, and for the sake of these one sins very much."[58] Intemperance is enkindled above all by the seductive glamor of the stimuli provided in an artificial civilization, with which the dishonorable team of blind lust and calculated greed surround the province of sexuality. All training and self-discipline aiming at chastity will find itself constantly faced with this situation. The resulting "overemphasis" on *temperantia* is in a certain sense fully justified (even though, on the other hand, the ethics of the so-called "fight against public immorality" seem to be a precarious and debatable business—and not only because of their ineffectiveness). Even St. Thomas assigns to *temperantia* primacy before fortitude and justice,—though in a circumscribed, non-actual sense,—since it must be most often proven in the world.[59]

We say in a circumscribed, non-actual sense, for the hierarchy which is actually and essentially valid is of a different kind.

But first a comment is necessary to avoid facile misunderstandings. In these considerations it is not a question of minimizing the gravity of the sins against chastity. No attempt at palliation can lessen the fearful weight of the willful turning of man from God. But we must never lose sight of the fact that the essential nature of sin lies exclusively in this willful turning away from God.[60] On the other hand, the opinion (again based on Tertullian) that unchastity is the gravest of all sins,[61] seems to base the gravity of this sin not so much on the turning away from God as on the turning of man to the goods of the sensual world; or, more directly and revealingly expressed: on defilement by a reality presumed to be impure and evil in its essence. St. Thomas, however, states that even a disordered turning of man to a transitory good, if it does not include a turning away from God, cannot be a mortal sin.[62]

But even the *Summa* once quotes the sentence of St. Isidore of Seville according to which the human race succumbs to the devil more through unchastity than in any other way.[63] In the moral teaching of the last hundred years this thought has played a dominant role, to an extent where it is overrefined to a definiteness of statement exceeding all human competence. For how could a mere human be able to know that—as a widely read theological writer of our times asserts—"there are ninety-nine people out of a hundred who will be damned for this very sin!"[64]

For St. Thomas, by contrast, the proposition of St. Isidore merely proved that in the sin of unchastity the compelling force of sensual desire is most effective; this very fact, however, mitigates the gravity of the sin, "because the sin is more venial the more overwhelming the sensual passion that drives one to it."[65]

But let us return to the consideration of the hierarchy of the virtues and the place of *temperantia* in that hierarchy. Over and over again Thomas has raised the question of the hierarchy of the virtues. His reply is as follows: "Man's good is rational good. But this good is possessed in its essence by prudence, which is the perfection of reason. But justice is the agent which makes this good real. It is the portion of justice to establish in all human affairs the order of reason. But the other virtues maintain and protect this good, insofar as they order the passions, lest these turn man away from rational good. In the hierarchy of these virtues fortitude has the first place. It is followed by temperance. That which concerns being is higher than that which concerns operation; and this again is higher than that which concerns maintenance and protection, in as much as only that which hinders is removed. Consequently, among the cardinal virtues prudence is the noblest; justice is the second, fortitude the third, *temperantia* the fourth."[66] "Justice and fortitude are higher virtues than temperance; but they are all exceeded by prudence and the theological virtues."[67]

Temperantia in its strict and ultimate sense is not

"realization" of the good.[68] Discipline, moderation, chastity do not in themselves constitute the perfection of man. By preserving and defending order in man himself, *temperantia* creates the indispensable prerequisite for both the realization of actual good and the actual movement of man toward his goal. Without it, the stream of the innermost human will-to-be would overflow destructively beyond all bounds, it would lose its direction, and never reach the sea of perfection. Yet *temperantia* is not itself the stream. But it is the shore, the banks, from whose solidity the stream receives the gift of straight unhindered course, of force, descent, and velocity.

III. VIRGINITY

THE NOBLE, truly princely practice of spending lavishly in order to make splendidly visible some sublime thought —either in a solemn celebration, in sculpture, or in architecture—this virtue (for it is a virtue!) the Middle Ages called *magnificentia*. We no longer can describe it in a single word. But the relation of *magnificentia* to ordinary generosity, which belongs to the daily sphere of needs and requests, is the same, says St. Thomas, as the relation of virginity to chastity.[1]

One might almost say that we lack today the right word for virginity also. For "virginity" designates in popular parlance the condition of intactness and singleness rather than the virtue, born of grace and resolve, of him who for the sake of God has forever renounced the experience of sexual enjoyment. Again we are constrained to think that this poverty of language must have its deepest cause in the fact that the popular mind is no longer deeply aware of the thing itself. However that may be, if here we briefly expound the nature of the virtue of *virginitas* under the name of virginity, we needs must keep in mind many discrepancies from current usages of speech and interpretation.

First: virginity is not a fact, but an act; not a condition, but a decision. That which constitutes virginity as a virtue is not mere inviolateness as a psychic (and certainly not as a physical) factor, even though this inviolateness may be the trophy of heroic chastity. Virginity as a virtue is established by the decision, or, to speak even more accurately, by the vow to refrain forever from sexual union and its attendant pleasure.

Nor is this all. Such a decision might spring from all sorts of reasons, for instance, from the anti-Christian view that this kind of abstinence is nothing but abstinence from evil.—Two things are involved in this decision, or rather enter into it and pervade it utterly.

First: "Virginity is honored not because it is virginity, but because it is consecrated."[2] The decision to live in sexual abstinence is not in itself worthy of praise; it is "made praiseworthy only by its end and purpose, to the extent that it aims to make him who practises it free for things divine."[3] It would be well if not only the non-Christian but the Christian also always kept in mind these two incontrovertible sentences of the greatest teachers of the Church, St. Augustine and St. Thomas, and remembered that consequently a virginity which does not realize the purpose of being free for God and for divine things becomes correspondingly meaningless and, in any case, loses the dignity for which it is honored by the Church. Of course, various chance necessities or even moral reasons may force or move a man to remain unmarried; and evidently the radiance of a sacrifice offered to God can be imparted to such a necessity or choice. But

84

to prize, on purely religious grounds, a celibacy that lacks the support of its most essential foundation, necessarily borders on Manichaeism, which regards the bare fact of celibacy itself as a good—and consequently sees something evil in marriage.

And here we come to the second fact expressed in the Christian decision to remain virginal: the affirmation of marriage as both a natural and a supernatural good. The Church has expressed this affirmation not only "where it belongs," that is, not only in the liturgy of the Nuptial Mass and in dogmatic decisions concerning the seventh sacrament. It is affirmed in the very prayer at the consecration of Virgins, where she speaks of the sanctity of matrimony and of the blessing that rests upon it; and in this very place virginity is expressly related to the same mystery that is included in the matrimonial union of man and wife.[4]

Only because of this mystery of the union with Christ, only because it fosters a more undivided devotion to God, is virginity superior to marriage. That virginity, chosen for the sake of a positive goal, really makes possible a fuller concentration need not be further discussed; it is evident to everybody that soldiers and political leaders remain freer for their tasks if they stay single.

On the other hand, however, we have the words of St. Catherine of Genoa, to a priest who spoke of the higher sanctity of the celibate life to her, who was a wife and a mother: Not even life in a military camp could distract her from her love of God—how much less, marriage! "If world or husband could hinder love, what a petty thing love would be!"[5]—With these refreshingly outspoken words the saint names not only the ultimate and decisive foundation of all sanctity (which, as St. Thomas teaches,[6] is not virginity, but love of God) but she also rightfully objects to the contrasting of the married and the virginal person (*in concreto*) as beings of different value, instead of the contrasting (*in abstracto*) of marriage and virginity. "Better the chastity of celibates than the chastity of the married; but I, the celibate, am not better than Abraham," says St. Augustine.[7] And in his book on virginity he admonishes virgins consecrated to God: "Whence does the virgin know, no matter how she may seek what is the Lord's, whether perhaps, for some weakness unknown to her, she is not yet ripe for the trial of martyrdom; and whether that married woman to whom she thinks herself superior may not already be able to drink the chalice of the Lord's suffering!"[8]

There are two, as it were, eternal objections to virginity: first, that it is against nature, and second, that by weakening the generative power of the people, it conflicts with the common weal. Only those ignorant of the range and acumen of St. Thomas's mind will be surprised to find both objections most precisely formulated in the *Summa Theologica*.[9]

More important still is his reply, built up in a three-membered argument.

First, the objection: As it is natural that man should give up his external goods—money and property—for the sake of his bodily health, so it is not contrary to nature that man renounce the gratification of physical desire for the sake of his spiritual and intellectual life. This is the natural order, appropriate to the nature of things and of man.—But how is this? No one would stop eating and drinking for the sake of spiritual goods, and is it not said in Holy Scripture: "Increase and multiply and people the earth!" (Genesis 1:28).

Second, the answer: There are two kinds of natural *must* and *may:* one is for the individual *I*, the other for the community of the *we*. Each individual *must* eat and drink. But the command of Genesis applies to the whole community of mankind. "In the army some keep watch over the camp, others are standard-bearers, and others fight with the sword. All these things are duties which make for community life which, in turn, cannot be carried out by the individual." It is consequently necessary for the human community "not only that it be propagated, but also that it flourish spiritually and intellectually. And therefore the common human weal has received its due if some fulfill the function of physical generation, while others, refraining from this, are entirely liberated for the contemplation of things divine—for the beauty and the salvation of the whole of mankind."[10]

Third, to clinch the argument: "The common weal is higher than the individual's, if both are of the same kind; but it may be that the good of the individual is of a higher kind. In this way virginity consecrated to God ranks higher than physical fertility."[11]

There are certain concepts which, as in a concave mirror, draw together a complete view of the world. And these same concepts are the crossroads where minds either meet or part. Of such is the concept of virginity.

Only he who recognizes the hierarchy which informs the three-membered argument of St. Thomas—namely, that the divine is infinitely higher than the human, and that the spiritual towers above the physical—who recognizes this hierarchy not only "conceptually" but "really" (to speak with Newman), he alone can comprehend the significance, the justification, and the dignity of virginity.

The notion and the actuality of the virginal life dedicated to God rise up like a sign of challenge. In this sign it becomes manifest whether the intellectual and spiritual goods really, validly, and vitally occupy their appropriate place and rank. In this sign also it becomes manifest whether these goods are counted among those by virtue of which the community of the people lives— "for the beauty and salvation of the whole of mankind."

IV. ON FASTING

Hilaritas mentis—cheerfulness of heart! Christian dogma links this notion most closely to the primal form of all asceticism, fasting.[1] This connection is based on the New Testament, on the Lord's admonition, proclaimed by the Church every year at the beginning of Lent: "When you fast, do not shew it by gloomy looks!" (Matt. 6:16).

St. Augustine says that it is quite indifferent what or how much a man eats, provided the welfare of those with whom he is associated, his own welfare and the requirements of health be not disregarded; what matters, he says, is just one thing, namely the ease and cheerfulness of heart with which he is able to renounce food if necessity or moral obligation require it.[2]

If necessity demands. This needs no elaboration. But what about fasting as a moral obligation? The reply leads us to the heart of the matter, and to a point of information that may greatly surprise modern Christians. We are inclined and accustomed to see in the practice of fasting a traditional and surely very meaningful custom of the Church; a custom which has somehow gathered obligatory force, but only by virtue of a purely disciplinary regulation of the Church, which is clearly ready to grant all kinds of alleviations and dispensations. Otherwise, fasting seems to us something extraordinary in every sense, linked at once to the idea of the ascetic and the saint. It is with some surprise, therefore, that we read in Aquinas, the "Universal Doctor of the Church," that fasting is a commandment of the natural law, quite specifically intended for the average Christian.[3] At this point it is important to recall that for St. Thomas the "natural law" is the fundamental source of obligation. The natural moral law is the ultimate "Ought," given and established directly in the nature of created reality, and as such endowed with supreme binding power. Consequently, the fasting regulations of the Church go back to this fundamental obligation, and constitute only a more accurately defined form, modified according to temporal circumstances and prevailing customs.[4]

Whoever has not reached the maturity of perfection —that is, all of us ordinary Christians—could not preserve, without recourse to the medicine, the discipline, of fasting, that inner order by virtue of which the turbulence of sensuality is kept in check and the spirit liberated so that it may soar into the zone of its appropriate fulfillment and satisfaction. It is here, most particularly and strikingly, that the stern demands inherent in the Christian image of man become compellingly visible. Our natural duty obliges us to pay dearly so that we may become what we are by essence: the free moral person in full possession of himself.

Everyone knows that, on the whole, the Church's laws of fasting are not taken too seriously. It would be an error, however, to attribute this primarily to contempt for the ecclesiastical authority. The reason for this laxity lies elsewhere, namely in the fact that nothing is as alien to the average Christian as the thought that there might be a natural, fundamental moral obligation to fast—before and apart from ecclesiastical injunctions. And many a priest would not be quite so ready to grant general mitigations of ecclesiastical rules of fasting were he to see in them not merely disciplinary regulations, but, with the "Universal Doctor," specific applications of a universal natural law.

Needless to say, this natural obligation to fast takes on a higher meaning and a deeper motivation from faith in Christ and from the supernatural love of God.[5] The theme of the perfection of nature through grace recurs here also. That perfection is represented in the very specifications which the "law of nature" experiences in the Church's rules of fasting.

The great fast of forty days, for instance, signifies that the Christian is preparing to share in the celebration of the mysteries of the death and resurrection of the Lord, wherein our redemption, which has its inception in the Incarnation, came finally to fruition. To obtain a share in these exalted realities demands in a special sense the prepared vessel of a free and "ordered" heart; on the other hand, no other reality, no other truth can so assuage and transform the innermost man.

"Can a man sin by fasting too strictly?" Nothing seems less pressing than this question, which heads one of the articles of St. Thomas.[6] But let it be noted in passing that he answers it affirmatively. For him, fasting is an act of *abstinentia*, an act of the virtue of abstinence, related, be it said, to the art of healing.[7] Again it is a question not of effort or castigation, but of the realization of the "order of reason."

With St. Jerome, St. Thomas says that to oppress one's body by exaggerated fasting and vigils is like bringing stolen goods as a sacrificial offering.[8] And in the *Summa Theologica*, we find the deeply Catholic thought that the Church, in her fasting regulations, is anxious also not to overtax nature, the natural will to live.[9] Characteristically, and not at all surprisingly, in the very article on fasting St. Thomas—who has been surnamed "Thomas of God the Creator"—mentions and refutes Manichaeism, his constant and primary adversary.[10] The following comments, also, should not be omitted here: "If one knowingly abstained from wine to the point of oppressing nature seriously, he would not be free of guilt;"[11] and: "For a man it is sinful to weaken his sexual potency by too strict fasting."[12] Admittedly, these propositions take no prominent place in St. Thomas's works—they are slipped in more or less in passing. But one might be tempted to mistake his thesis on the natural obligation to fast for stark, unrelieved asceticism, were it not for these bright sparks of affirmation. Nonetheless, the validity of this thesis retains its full force.

Transgressions against the virtue of *abstinentia,* that is, against the "rational order" in the sphere of enjoyment of food and drink, are apt to be taken very lightly, if they are subjected to moral judgment at all. But to one who holds for a clear, decisive affirmation of the Christian image of man, the destructive effect of an obsessive pre-occupation with the what and how much of food and drink is perfectly obvious. St. Thomas calls this effect *hebetudo sensus*[13]—the dulling and obscuring of the inner perception of spiritual realities. And might there not be a causal connection between this by now customary and fully accepted phenomenon of the dullness of inner perception, and the equally accepted and customary laxity? We might find cause for reflection in the wisdom of the Orient.

In Dante's cosmological poem, we find, in the second of the three cantos of the *Purgatorio* which treat of abstaining from the "gratification of the palate," an extremely striking, indeed a quite disconcerting, stanza. It says of the penitents: "The sockets of their eyes seemed rings without gems. Whoso in the face of men reads OMO, would surely there have recognized the M."[14] What is implied here is nothing less than this: through the penance of fasting, that which was devastated by the "gratification of the palate" is restored, namely, the inner form of man.

But to return once more to "cheerfulness of heart": Fasting should be performed with a cheerful heart. This is, as it were, a polemical exhortation. Christ himself has named its counterpart "the disfigured faces of the hypocrites." And the experience of the ascetics furnishes another obverse.

All discipline, we have said, has reference to the operating person. This reference, however, bears in itself the constant danger of the loss of self-detachment, and of a change into self-righteousness, which draws from its ascetic "achievements" the profit of a solid self-admiration. Vanity, self-importance, impatient arrogance rising superior to the "imperfect"—these are the specific perils of the ascetic. Gregory the Great points this out clearly in his "Rule for Pastors," an inexhaustible treasure house of practical wisdom.[15]

Cheerfulness of heart, however, is the mark of selflessness. By this sign and seal one is sure to recognize that hypocrisy and all manner of tense self-involvement are done away with. Cheerfulness of heart is the infallible token that reveals the inner genuineness of discipline as *selfless* preservation of the self.

V. THE SENSE OF TOUCH

St. Thomas says that *temperantia* has reference above all to the pleasure assigned to the sense of touch.[1] And to this sense are assigned both sexual pleasure and the pleasures of eating and drinking.[2]

We are too apt to take these statements with false literalness and to misinterpret them to the point of excessive triviality. Therefore it is necessary to point out briefly that they have a depth of bearing unsuspected at first glance, and why this is so.

The sense of touch, according to St. Thomas (and Aristotle) has a special rank among the senses. It is not a sense among other senses, but is the "basis of the other senses;"[3] "all other senses are based on the sense of touch."[4] In this sense of touch there is contained principially the entire essence of the senses in general.[5] By the sense of touch, above all, a being becomes sentient—*animal*;[6] where there is no sense of touch, there is no sentient life.[7]—This is the first point.

Second: "Among all sentient creatures man has the best sense of touch."[8] "There are animals which see more sharply or hear more acutely or smell more intensely than man. In the sense of touch, however, man differs from all other sentient beings by having a much more acute perception."[9]

And third: "Among men themselves those who possess the better sense of touch have the better power of cognition."[10] "One might suppose that cognitive talent should rather correspond to the excellence of the sense of sight than to that of touch, as the sense of sight is the intellectual sense and best perceives differences in things. . . . But one must say that cognitive talent corresponds more to the excellence of the sense of touch because the sense of touch is the basis of all other senses. Therefore he who has the better sense of touch has consequently simply a more sensitive nature and as a result a keener intelligence. For the excellence of sensitivity is the basis of excellence of intelligence. But from the fact that one has a better auditory or a better visual sense it does not follow that he is simply more sensitive; at most this is so only in a certain respect."[11]

These three thoughts, as surprising to come upon as a treasure trove, are here merely quoted and not commented on. For the purpose of this book, it is of no importance what modern sensorial physiology, for instance, would say to this. A look into the manuals will show that the basic approach in both the questions and the replies of St. Thomas is so immeasurably removed from today's notions that they cannot even be said to contradict each other.

But it is important to recognize that according to St.

Thomas, the virtue of temperance, especially in its primordial forms of chastity and abstinence, relates to the root of the whole of sensual-intellectual life. Moderation extends its ordering mastery down to the fountainhead from which the figure of moral man springs up unceasingly.

Still another connection, hidden up to now, becomes visible in the conceptual field of relations pertaining to moderation.

The sense of touch is also the organ of pain.[12] And mastery of the spirit over pleasure linked with the sense of touch equally signifies mastery over pain.

Discipline, says Ernst Jünger in his notable essay "Concerning Pain," has no other significance than this: to keep life in constant contact with pain and by this means in readiness "to be sacrificed for the purpose of a higher order."[13]

Needless to say that the mask-like rigidity of Jünger's concept of "discipline" is essentially different from the Christian concept of temperance and moderation. Jünger would never have been able to endorse St. Thomas's proposition: "The goal and norm of temperance is blessedness."[14] And yet, if we regard the Christian notion of temperance from the angle of pain, a sterner face rises behind the foreground of creational joy, a face molded by the decision to relinquish the created for the sake of the Creator. But this sterner face, also, radiates an assenting joy, immeasurably above all ingenuous rejoicing in the created.

97

VI. HUMILITY

ONE OF THE GOODS in which man naturally seeks fulfillment of his being is *excellentia:* superiority, pre-eminence,
consideration.[1] The virtue of temperance, insofar as it relates this natural urge to the order of reason, is called
humility. The ground of humility is man's estimation of
himself according to truth.[2] And that is almost all there
is to it.

Starting from this definition, it is difficult to understand how "humility" could have become, as it were, a
bone of contention. To disregard the demonic resistance
against good which makes this feature of the Christian
image of man its particular target, is possible only because
the notion of humility has become blurred even in the
Christian consciousness. In the whole tractate of St.
Thomas concerning humility and pride, there is not a
single sentence to suggest an attitude, on principle, of
constant self-accusation, of disparagement of one's being
and doing, of cringing inferiority feelings, as belonging
to humility or any other Christian virtue.

Nothing lights the way to a proper understanding of
humility more tellingly than this: humility and high-

mindedness not only are not mutually exclusive,³ but actually are neighbors and akin; and both are equally opposed to either pride or pusillanimity.⁴

What is meant by high-mindedness or magnanimity? It is the striving of the mind toward great things.⁵ High-minded is the man who feels the potentiality of greatness and prepares for it. The high-minded or magnanimous man is, in a certain sense, "selective." He will not be accessible to every approach, but will keep himself for the greatness to which he feels akin.⁶ Above all, high-mindedness is demanding as to honor: "The high-minded man strives toward that which deserves the highest honor."⁷ In the *Summa Theologica* we read: "If a man should despise honor to the extent that he would not take care to do what is deserving of honor, this would be blameworthy."⁸ On the other hand, the high-minded man is not crushed by dishonor; he disregards it as something beneath him.⁹ The high-minded man despises everything small-minded. He would never prize another man so highly as to do anything improper for his sake.¹⁰ The words of the Psalmist (Psalm 14:4): "The evil-doer is nothing in his sight," refer to the high-minded "contempt of men" of the just, says St. Thomas.¹¹ Fearless frankness is the hallmark of high-mindedness; nothing is further from it than to suppress truth from fear.¹² Flattery and dissimulation are equally removed from the high-minded.¹³ The high-minded man does not complain; for his heart is impervious to external evil.¹⁴ High-mindedness implies an unshakable firmness of hope, an actually challenging assurance,¹⁵ and the perfect peace of a fearless heart.[16] The high-minded man bows neither to confusion of the soul, nor to any man, nor to fate—but to God alone.[17]

One marvels to learn that this description of high-mindedness is drawn, trait by trait, in the *Summa Theologica* of Aquinas. This needed to be made clear. For in the treatise on humility it is said repeatedly that humility is not opposed to high-mindedness. Now we can fathom the true significance of this statement, spoken as if it were a warning and a caution. This is its meaning: a "humility" too weak and too narrow to be able to bear the inner tension of cohabitation with high-mindedness is not true humility.

The customary judgment of men is always prone to call a high-minded man a haughty man, and so equally to miss the true nature of humility. "A haughty man"— this is easily and quickly said. But only rarely is the quality here implied that of pride (*superbia*). Pride is not, in the first place, a quality of everyday behavior in human relationships. Pride refers to man's relationship to God. Pride is the anti-realistic denial of the relationship between creature and Creator; pride denies the creaturely nature of man. Every sin contains two elements: a turning away from God and a turning toward transitory good; the decisive and defining element is the first one: the turning away from God. And this is more pronounced in pride than in any other sin. "All sins flee before God; pride alone stands up against God."[18] Holy Scripture says of the proud alone that "God flouts the scornful" (Jas. 4:6).

Humility, too, is not primarily an attitude in human relationships. Humility, too, looks first to God. That which pride denies and destroys, humility affirms and preserves: the creaturely quality of man. If to be a creature—to be created—is the innermost nature of man, then humility, as "subjection of man to God,"[19] is the affirmation of this essential and primordial fact. Second: Humility, consequently, is not outward behavior but an inner attitude, born of decision of the will.[20] Regarding God and its own creaturely quality, it is an attitude of perfect recognition of that which, by reason of God's will, really *is;* above all, it is candid acceptance of this one thing: that man and humanity are neither God nor "like God." At this point we get a glimpse of the hidden connection that links the Christian virtue of humility with the—perhaps equally Christian—gift of humor.

Third, and finally: Can we avoid stating outright that beyond everything said so far, humility is also an attitude of man to man, namely the attitude of self-abasement of one before the other? Let us examine this more closely.

In the *Summa Theologica*, St. Thomas specifically raises the question of the humble attitude of man to man, and answers it as follows: "In man, two things have to be considered: that which is of God, and that which is of man. . . . But humility in the strict sense means the awe in virtue of which man subjects himself to God. Consequently man, with regard to that which is of himself, must subject himself to his neighbor with regard to that which is of God in him. But humility does not require

that one subject that which is of God in himself to that
which seems to be of God in the other. . . . Humility
likewise does not require that one subject that which is of
himself to that which is of man in the other."[21]

In the broad and many-graded area of this reply there
is room for the "contempt of men" on the part of the
high-minded just as there is for the self-abasement of St.
Francis of Assisi, who took off his cowl and had himself
brought before the people with a rope around his neck.[22]
Here again it becomes evident that Christian teaching is
wary of the tightness and confinement of one-track rules.
This caution, or, better, aversion is voiced by St. Augustine in another though related reference: "If one man
says you should not receive the Eucharist every day, and
another says the opposite, let each one do what he thinks
he should, in piety, according to his own belief. For
neither did Zacchæus and the Roman officer dispute with
one another, although the one received the Lord with joy
into his house and the other said: 'I am not worthy that
thou shouldst enter under my roof' (Luke 19:6; 7:6).
Both honored the Redeemer, though not in the same
manner."[23]

VII. THE POWER OF WRATH

IN CHRISTIAN PARLANCE, the notions of "sensuality," "passion," "desire" are customarily—though very unjustly—understood exclusively as "anti-spiritual sensuality," "wicked passion," "rebellious desire." Such a constriction of an originally much broader meaning obscures the important fact that all these notions by no means have a merely negative sense; rather, they represent forces from which the essence of human nature is built up and draws its life. The same is true of the notion of wrath or anger. At the mention of anger, Christian awareness sees as a rule only the uncontrolled, the anti-spiritual, the negative aspect. But, as with "sensuality" and "desire," the power of wrath also belongs to the primal forces of human nature. In this power of wrath, the energy of human nature is most clearly expressed. It is a force directed toward the difficult of achievement, toward the thing beyond the easy grasp, ever ready to expose itself wherever an "arduous good" waits to be conquered. "The power of anger is given to sentient beings so that the hindrances may be removed whereby the force of desire is impeded from striving toward its object, whether because of the difficulty of achieving a good or because of the difficulty of overcoming an evil."[1] Wrath is the strength to attack the repugnant;[2] the power of anger is actually the power of resistance in the soul.[3]

Whoever, therefore, stigmatizes the power of wrath as something in itself anti-spiritual and consequently to be "mortified" is committing the same error as one who similarly slights "sensuality," "passion" and "desire." Both contemn the basic forces of our being; both are offending the Creator, Who, as the liturgy of the Church says, has "marvellously established the dignity of human nature."

Concerning wrath (in the narrower sense), understood as the passionate desire for just retribution of injustice that has been suffered, St. Thomas, in repudiation of the Stoics, says the following: "Because the nature of man is constructed of soul and body, of spirit and sensuality, it belongs to the good of man to devote himself *utterly* to virtue, namely with spirit, sensuality, and body alike. And therefore man's virtue requires that the will for just retribution reside not only in the spiritual realm of the soul, but also in sensuality and in the body itself." This passage is found in the great work of St. Thomas's later life, the *De Malo*, in an article discussing the question "whether all wrath is evil."[4] Anger is "good" if, in accordance with the order of reason, it is brought into service for the true goals of man;[5] one who does good with passion is more praiseworthy than one who is "not entirely" afire for the good, even to the forces of the sensual realm.[6] Gregory the Great says: "Reason opposes evil the more effectively when anger ministers at her side."[7] And what was said of the power of sexual desire, which overwhelms reason, is likewise true of the obscuring power of anger: "It is not contrary to the nature of virtue that the consideration of reason comes to a stop in the execution of that which reason has already considered; even art would be impeded in its activity if it should wish to consider what was to be done where it was a question of immediate action."[8]

The surprise with which we reflect on these statements makes us aware once again how far we are from considering the whole man in our conception of the moral good. We realize how much we almost unconsciously tend to take the "purely spiritual" for actual humanity; how much, on the other hand, the "ancients" can teach us and make us once again embrace the full created nature of world and man, in its true reality.

It is self-evident that the anger which breaks all bounds and disrupts the order of reason is evil and is sin. Blind wrath, bitterness of spirit, and revengeful resentment, the three basic forms of intemperate anger,[9] are therefore evil and contrary to order.

Blind wrath shuts the eyes of the spirit before they have been able to grasp the facts and to judge them; bitterness and resentment, with a grim joy in negation, close their ears to the language of truth and love;[10] they poison the heart like a festering ulcer.[11] Also evil, of course, is all anger linked to unjust desire. This needs no further discussion.

In the upsurge of his self-will, the intemperately angry man feels as if he were drawing his whole being together like a club ready to strike. But this is the very thing he fails to achieve. Only gentleness and mildness can accomplish it. (The two are not equivalent; mildness is gentleness turned toward what is without.[12]) "Gentleness above all makes man master of himself."[13] Holy Scripture speaks of this virtue in much the same terms as of patience. In St. Luke's Gospel, it is said of patience that through it man possesses his soul; and of gentleness it is said: "Possess thy soul through gentleness" (Eccles. 10:31).

Gentleness, however, does not signify that the original power of wrath is weakened or, worse still, "mortified," just as chastity does not imply a weakening of sexual power. On the contrary: gentleness as a virtue presupposes the power of wrath; gentleness implies mastery of this power, not its weakening. We should not mistake the pale-faced harmlessness which pretends to be gentleness—unfortunately often successfully—for a Christian virtue. Lack of sensuality is not chastity; and incapacity for wrath has nothing to do with gentleness. Such incapacity not only is not a virtue, but, as St. Thomas expressly says, a fault: *peccatum* and *vitium*.[14]

In the *Summa Theologica*, St. Thomas raises and answers a remarkable question: Which is the greater evil and wrong: intemperateness in wrath, or intemperateness in pleasure?[15] His reply is: If we consider the fruits of

each, it is intemperate wrath that is, as a rule, the greater
evil, as it commonly works against the welfare of one's
neighbor. But if we consider the passion itself, which in
both cases degenerates into intemperateness, then intemperate pleasure is the greater wrong, for various reasons.
The excitement of anger, for example, since it is aroused
by an injustice, still in some way appertains to reason;
whereas pleasure refers exclusively to sensuality. Speaking absolutely, the sin of intemperate wrath is less evil
than intemperate pleasure, in the same proportion as the
good of justice toward which the angry man is directed
ranks above the pleasure-seeking of the lustful man. This,
also, is the reason why the intemperately lustful man is
more contemptible than the immoderately angry one.[16]
Further, immoderate wrath is as a rule conditioned by
the physical constitution—that is, by natural disposition
—more than immoderate pleasure-seeking. (For this reason, the inclination to immoderate anger is more easily
and frequently hereditary than that of immoderate pleasure-seeking.) And finally, the intemperately wrathful
man is less obnoxious than the intemperately lustful one,
because the former, akin to the high-minded, is all frankness, while the immoderate pleasure-seeker, intent on dissimulation and camouflage, is unable to give or take a
straight look in the eye.

It is particularly in reference to overcoming intemperateness of sensual desire that the power of wrath acquires a special importance.

Aquinas, it is true, also says that an acute temptation

to unchastity is most easily conquerable by flight.[17] But he likewise knows that the addiction to degenerate pleasure-seeking can by no means be cured through a merely negative approach, through convulsively "shutting one's mind" to it. Thomas believes that the deterioration of one power of the soul should be healed and supplemented by the still undamaged core of some other power. Thus it should be possible to subdue and, as it were, to quench the limp intemperateness of an unchaste lustfulness by attacking a difficult task with the resilient joy generated in the full power of wrath.[18]

Only the combination of the intemperateness of lustfulness with the lazy inertia incapable of generating anger is the sign of complete and virtually hopeless degeneration. It appears whenever a caste, a people, or a whole civilization is ripe for its decline and fall.

VIII. DISCIPLINING THE EYES

THAT THE WORDS *studiositas* and *curiositas* were not translated at their first mention was not unintentional nor indeed without necessity. Of course it would be easy enough to render them, following the dictionary, as "desire for knowledge" or "zeal," for the first, and "inquisitiveness," for the second. But this would amount to suppressing their most important meaning. Further, one might think that we speak but trivially and condescendingly of the virtue of the "good student" and of the more or less harmless weakness of the woman gossiping across the back fence.

Studiositas, curiositas—by these are meant temperateness and intemperance, respectively, in the natural striving for knowledge; temperateness and intemperance, above all, in the indulgence of the sensual perception of the manifold sensuous beauty of the world; temperateness and intemperance in the "desire for knowledge and experience," as St. Augustine puts it.[1]

Nietzsche said that wisdom "puts limits to knowledge." Whatever he himself may have meant by this, there is no doubt that the will-to-knowledge, this noble power of the human being, requires a restraining wisdom, "in order that man may not strive immoderately for the knowledge of things."[2]

But in what consists such immoderateness? Certainly not (as has been said by St. Thomas, in refutation of the scorners of natural creation, and as we must repeat today, addressing ourselves to the same tendencies) in the fact that the mind of man strives to unseal the natural secrets and locked places of creation: consequently not in "secular science" *per se*. Concerning the study of philosophy, for instance, we read in the *Summa Theologica* that it is "to be praised for the truth which was recognized by the (pagan) philosophers, namely, as the Epistle to the Romans says (1:19) because God revealed it to them."[3]

All the same, in view of the armed attack upon the natural mysteries of creation, it would be well to keep in mind the startling phrase of the aged Goethe: "We would have a better knowledge of things if we did not try to know them so thoroughly."[4]

Immoderateness in striving for knowledge, says St. Thomas, is exemplified in magic.[5] Nowadays, this thought makes us smile. But are we really so far removed from being willing to pay the price even of our salvation for the unlocking of impenetrabilities, should the choice be open to us—that is the question. Further, it is also immoderate and senseless to try and master God Himself and His work by deciphering His intentions. We may, for instance, be able to grasp in faith the actuality and the ultimate meaning of God's working in history. But no man can presume on his own to point to any providential happening of the here and now, and to say: "God has manifested his intention in this or that reward or punishment, confirmation or rejection." This temptation to unveil God's incomprehensibility for tangible everyday use, thereby negating it, is concealed under a thousand disguises and is equally close and perilous for the most profound as for the most superficial minds. St. Augustine writes in his *Confessions:* "Indeed, I no longer trouble myself about the course of the stars, and my soul hath never sought an answer from the shades; I condemn all this blasphemous magic. But how hath the Enemy seduced me with his thousandfold wiles that I, O Lord my God, should require a sign from Thee, whom I should serve all loyally and simply!"

The essential intemperateness of the urge for knowledge, however, is "concupiscence of the eyes." Only by working through a tangled thicket of vague and false interpretation, and by following the guidance of St. Augustine and St. Thomas, can we obtain a grasp of the true significance of this word of Scripture. It has, as will be seen, an immediate relevance to modern man.

There is a gratification in seeing that reverses the original meaning of vision and works disorder in man himself. The true meaning of seeing is perception of reality. But "concupiscence of the eyes" does not aim to perceive reality, but to enjoy "seeing." St. Augustine says of the "concupiscence of the palate" that it is not a question of satiating one's hunger but of tasting and relishing food;[7] this is also true of *curiositas* and the "concupiscence of the eyes." "What this seeing strives for is not to attain knowledge and to become cognizant with the truth, but for possibilities of relinquishing oneself to the world," says Heidegger in his book *Sein und Zeit*.[8]

Aquinas assigns *curiositas* to the "roaming unrest of spirit," *evagatio mentis*, which he says is the first-born daughter of *acedia*. Since these interrelations are anything but constructions of a game of allegories, it is well worth to give them a moment's closer scrutiny. *Acedia* is the dreary sadness of a heart unwilling to accept the greatness to which man is called by God; this inertia raises its paralyzing face wherever man is trying to shake off the obligatory nobility of being that belongs to his essential dignity as a person, and particularly the nobility of the sonship of God, thus denying his true self.[9] *Acedia*, says Thomas, first shows its effect in the "roaming unrest of the spirit."[10] (Its second daughter is despair and this kinship throws revealing sidelights on the subject of our present discussion.) "Roaming unrest of the spirit," on the other hand, manifests itself in verbosity, in unbridled desire "to burst forth from the citadel of the spirit into diversity"; in inner restlessness, in instability of place as well as instability of resolution, and especially in the insatiability of *curiositas*.[11]

Accordingly, the degeneration into *curiositas* of the natural wish to see may be much more than a harmless confusion on the surface of the human being. It may be the sign of complete rootlessness. It may mean that man has lost his capacity for living with himself; that, in flight from himself, nauseated and bored by the void of an interior life gutted by despair, he is seeking with selfish anxiety and on a thousand futile paths that which is given only to the noble stillness of a heart held ready for sacrifice and thus in possession of itself, namely, the fullness of being. Because he is not really living from the wellspring of his nature, he seeks, as Heidegger says, in "curiosity, to which nothing remains closed," the pledge of a supposedly genuine "living Life."[12]

Not for nothing does Holy Scripture name "concupiscence of the eyes" among the three powers which constitute the world that "lieth in the power of evil" (I John 2:16; 5:19).

It reaches the extremes of its destructive and eradicating power when it builds itself a world according to its own image and likeness: when it surrounds itself with the restlessness of a perpetual moving picture of meaningless shows, and with the literally deafening noise of impressions and sensations breathlessly rushing past the windows of the senses. Behind the flimsy pomp of its façade dwells absolute nothingness; it is a world of, at most, ephemeral creations, which often within less than a quarter hour become stale and discarded, like a newspaper or magazine swiftly scanned or merely perused; a world which, to the piercing eye of the healthy mind untouched by its contagion, appears like the amusement quarter of a big city in the hard brightness of a winter morning: desperately bare, disconsolate, and ghostly.

The destructiveness of this disorder which originates from, and grows upon, obsessive addiction, lies in the fact that it stifles man's primitive power of perceiving reality; that it makes man incapable not only of coming to himself but also of reaching reality and truth.

If such an illusory world threatens to overgrow and smother the world of real things, then to restrain the natural wish to see takes on the character of a measure of self-protection and self-defense. *Studiositas*, in this frame of reference, primarily signifies that man should oppose this virtually inescapable seduction with all the force of selfless self-preservation; that he should hermetically close the inner room of his being against the intrusively boisterous pseudo-reality of empty shows and sounds. It is in such an asceticism of cognition alone that he may preserve or regain that which actually constitutes man's vital existence: the perception of the reality of God and His creation, and the possibility of shaping himself and the world according to this truth, which reveals itself only in silence.

IX. THE FRUITS OF TEMPERANCE

To the virtue of temperance as the preserving and defending realization of man's inner order, the gift of beauty is particularly coordinated. Not only is temperance beautiful in itself, it also renders men beautiful.[1] Beauty, however, must here be understood in its original meaning: as the glow of the true and the good irradiating from every ordered state of being, and not in the patent significance of immediate sensual appeal. The beauty of temperance has a more spiritual, more austere, more virile aspect. It is of the essence of this beauty that it does not conflict with true virility, but rather has an affinity to it. Temperance, as the wellspring and premise of fortitude,[2] is the virtue of mature manliness.

The infantile[3] disorder of intemperance, on the other hand, not only destroys beauty,[4] it also makes man cowardly; intemperance more than any other thing renders man unable and unwilling to "take heart" against the wounding power of evil in the world.[5]

It is not easy to read in a man's face whether he is just or unjust. Temperance or intemperance, however, loudly proclaim themselves in everything that manifests a personality: in the order or disorder of the features, in

the attitude, the laugh, the handwriting. Temperance, as
the inner order of man, can as little remain "purely interior" as the soul itself, and as all other life of the soul
or mind. It is the nature of the soul to be the "form of
the body."

This fundamental principle of all Christian psychology[6] not only states the in-forming of the body by
the soul, but also the reference of the soul to the body.
On this, a second factor is based: temperance or intemperance of outward behavior and expression can have
its strengthening or weakening repercussion on the inner
order of man.[7] It is from this point of view that all outer
discipline—whether in the sphere of sexual pleasure or in
that of eating and drinking, of self-assertion, of anger,
and of the gratification of the eye—obtains its meaning,
its justification, and its necessity.

It is a noteworthy fact—but who has ever called attention to it?—that almost all pathological obsessions,
witnesses as they are to a disturbed inner order, belong to
the sphere of *temperantia*: sexual aberrations as well as
dipsomania, delusion of grandeur, pathological irasci-
bility, and the passive craving of the rootless for sensations. All these petrifactions of selfishness are accom-
panied by the despair of missing the goal striven for with
such violent exertion of will—namely the gratification of
the self. In the nature of things, all selfish self-seeking is
a desperate effort. For it is a natural, primal fact, prior to
all human decision, that man loves God more than himself, and consequently that he must of necessity miss his

very goal—himself—by following the ungodly, the "anti-godly," path of selfishness.

Intemperantia and despair are connected by a hidden channel. Whoever in stubborn recklessness persists in pursuing perfect satisfaction and gratification in prestige and pleasure has set his foot on the road to despair. Another thing, also, is true: one who rejects fulfillment in its true and final meaning, and, despairing of God and himself, anticipates non-fulfillment,[8] may well regard the artificial paradise of unrestrained pleasure-seeking as the sole place, if not of happiness, then of forgetfulness, of self-oblivion: "In their despair, they gave themselves up to incontinence" (Ephesians 4:19).[9]

That sin is a burden and a bondage is nowhere more apparent than in *intemperantia*, in that obsession of selfish self-preservation, which seeks itself in vain.

Temperance, on the contrary, is liberating and puri-fying. This above all: temperance effects purification.

If one approaches the difficult concept of purity through this strangely neglected gateway and begins to understand purity as the fruit of purification, the confusing and discordant sounds which usually obscure this notion and move it dangerously close to Manichaeism are silenced. From this approach the full and unrestricted concept of purity—so different from the currently accepted one—comes into view.

This is the purity meant by John Cassian when he calls purity of heart the immanent purpose of temperance: "It is served by solitude, fasting, night watches, and penitence."[10] It is this wider concept of purity which is referred to in St. Augustine's statement that the virtue of temperance and moderation aims at preserving man uninjured and undefiled for God.[11]

But what does this unrestricted concept of purity stand for? It stands for that crystal-clear, morning-fresh freedom from self-consciousness, for that selfless acceptance of the world which man experiences when the shock of a profound sorrow carries him to the brink of existence or when he is touched by the shadow of death. It is said in the Scriptures: "Grave illness sobers the soul" (Eccles. 31:2); this sobriety belongs to the essence of purity. That most disputed statement of Aristotle: tragedy causes purification, catharsis,[12] points in the same direction. Even the Holy Spirit's gift of fear, which St. Thomas assigns to *temperantia*,[13] purifies the soul by causing it to experience, through grace, the innermost peril of man. Its fruit is that purity by dint of which the selfish and furtive search for spurious fulfillment is abandoned. Purity is the perfect unfolding of the whole nature from which alone could have come the words: "Behold the handmaid of the Lord!" (Luke 1:38).

A new depth here opens to our view: purity is not only the fruit of purification; it implies at the same time readiness to accept God's purifying intervention, terrible and fatal though it might be; to accept it with the bold candor of a trustful heart, and thus to experience its fruitful and transforming power.

This then is the ultimate meaning of the virtue of temperance.

NOTES

In the following Notes, the quotations from the *Summa Theologica* of St. Thomas Aquinas are indicated only by ciphers; "II, II, 125, 2 ad 2" stands for *Summa Theologica*, second part of the second part, question 125, article 2, answer to the second objection. For quotations from the *Commentary on the Sentences* only arabic numbers are used: "3, d. 33, 2, 5" stands for third book, distinction 33, question 2, article 5. Titles of other works of St. Thomas are abbreviated as follows:

Summa contra Gentes, C.G.
Commentary on Aristotle's "On the Soul," In An.
Commentary on the Second Epistle to the Corinthians, In II Cor.
Commentary on the Epistle to the Romans, In Rom.
Expositio in Evangelium B. Joannis, In John
Quaestio disputata de anima, An.
Quaestio disputata de virtutibus cardinalibus, Virt. card.
Quaestio disputata de virtutibus in communis, Virt. comm.
Quaestiones disputatae de malo, Mal.
Quaestiones disputatae de veritate, Ver.
Quaestiones quodlibetales, Quol.

FORTITUDE

I

1. Mal. 1, 4
2. Carl Schmitt, *Der Begriff des Politischen,* Hamburg, 1933,
   p. 44
3. II, II, 141, 8
4. St. Augustine, *The City of God,* 19, 4

II

1. Quol. 4, 20
2. *Martyrdom of St. Polycarp*, 4
3. *The Proconsular Acts of St. Cyprian*, 1
4. II, II, 123, 8
5. *Serm.* 16; quoted in II, II, 124, 4, sed contra
6. Tertullian, *Apologeticum*, 50
7. II, II, 123, 8

III

1. II, II, 125, 2 ad 2
2. *Virt. card.* 4 ad 5
3. II, II, 124, 3
4. II, II, 123, 12 ad 2
5. *De officiis* 1, 35
6. 3, d. 33, 2, 5
7. Ver. 14, 5 ad II; 3, d. 27, 2, 4, 3
8. *Virt. card.* 1
9. *Virt. comm.* 12 ad 23
10. II, II, 129, 5 ad 2
11. II, II, 126, 2 ad 1
12. Thucydides, *Peloponnesian War*, Book II
13. II, II, 123, 12
14. *Enarrationes in Psalmos* 34, 13
15. II, II, 123, 12 ad 3
16. *De officiis* I, 35

IV

1. II, II, 123, 1 ad 2
2. II, II, 123, 4
3. II, II, 123, 6
4. II, II, 123, 6 ad 2
5. II, II, 136, 4 ad 2
6. I, II, 66, 4 ad 2; II, II, 128, 1

7. II, II, 128, 1
8. Scivias III, 22
9. II, II, 136, 2 ad 2
10. I, II, 66, 4 ad 2; *Virt. card.* 1 ad 4
11. II, II, 128, 1 ad 2
12. II, II, 123, 10 ad 3
13. St. Athanasius, *Third Oration against the Arians,* chap. 57
14. In John 18, lect. 4, 2

V

1. Fritz Künkel, *Neurasthenie und Hysterie; Handbuch der Individualpsychologie* (ed. E. Wexberg; Munich, 1926) p. 500
2. I, II, 68, 2
3. I, II, 62, 5
4. I, II, 62, 5
5. II, II, 159, 2 ad 1
6. St. Teresa of Avila, *Autobiography,* chap. 31, 18
7. II, II, 139, 1
8. This work is based upon the theology of St. Thomas Aquinas and St. John of the Cross

TEMPERANCE

I

1. 4, d. 14, 1, 1, 4 ad 2; II, II, 141, 2, obj. 2
2. II, II, 141, 8
3. *Virt. card.* 4; I, II, 61, 5
4. II, II, 141, 2 ad 2
5. 1, 60, 5
6. II, II, 23, 7
7. E. Przywara, *Das Geheimnis Kierkegaards,* Munich, 1929, p. 77 f.
8. II, II, 141, 4
9. II, II, 161; 162
10. II, II, 157; 158

11. II, II, 166; 167

II

1. Mal. 15, 2
2. "As the use of foods can be without sin, if it be done in a proper manner and order, according to what befits bodily health: thus also the use of sex can be without any sin, if it be done in a proper manner and order, according to what is suitable to the purpose of human propagation." II, II, 153, 2
3. Ibid.
4. II, II, 142,1; 152, 2 ad 2; 153, 3 ad 3
5. 4, d.33,1,1
6. *Twelfth Homily on the Epistle to the Colossians.* I owe this quotation to the excellent book of August Adam, *Der Primat der Liebe*, Kevelaer, no date.
7. II, II, 153, 3
8. II, II, 151, 1
9. II, II, 153, 3; 154, 1
10. Cf. Josef Pieper, *Die Wirklichkeit und das Gute*, Leipzig, 1935, p.84f.
11. II, II, 153, 3 ad 2
12. Cf. also II, II, 152, 2; 146, 1 ad 1
13. II, II, 151, 4
14. I, II, 18, 5
15. II, II, 153, obj. 2, ad 2
16. I, 98, 2
17. I, 98, 2 ad 3
18. II, II, 154, 1 ad 2
19. II, II, 153, 3; Mal. 15, 2 ad 4
20. II, II, 122, 1; 122,6
21. II, II, 154, 2
22. II, II, 153, 5 ad 1
23. Ibid.
24. II, II, 15, 3
25. II, II, 53, 6 ad 2
26. II, II, 180, 2 ad 3
27. II, II, 155, 1 ad 2

28. *Enarrationes in psalmos* 72, 32
29. Mal. 15, 4: (*ratio*), *secundum quod dirigit humanos actus:* (reason), in accordance with the fact that it directs human actions.
30. II, II, 153, 5 ad 1
31. Cf. *Die Wirklichkeit und das Gute*, p. 53ff.
32. Mal. 15, 4
33. II, II, 155, 4; 156, 3
34. II, II, 155, 4 ad 3
35. II, II, 155, 4; *Virt. card.* 1 ad 6; II, II, 123, 12 ad 2
36. *Nicomachaean Ethics*, 7, 9 (1151a)
37. II, II, 156, 3 ad 1
38. II, II, 156, 3
39. Ibid.
40. Mal. 3, 13
41. Ibid.
42. Cf. Aristotle, *Nicomachaean Ethics, loc. cit.*
43. I, II, 64, 2
44. *Somme théologique*, La tempérance, tome 2, Paris, 1928, p.324
45. II, II, 170, 1 ad 3
46. Quol. 12, 33
47. II, II, 154, 4; Ver. 15, 4
48. I cannot recall having run across the expression *partes inhonestae* (indecent parts) anywhere in the writings of St. Thomas. Yet this expression, very suspicious in itself, might have some meaning in regard to man, if used with the necessary reservations (cf. Lactantius, *De opificio Dei,* 13); namely that the constant possibility of a rebellion of the senses against the spirit becomes most likely and most obvious in the generative organs (II, II, 154, 4). But the expression becomes completely meaningless when referring to an animal. It may also be noted that such a book as the *Vademecum theologiae moralis* (Handbook of Moral Theology) by Fr. Prümmer, O.Praem. (Freiburg, 1921), which, despite its usually strong reliance on the structure of the second part of the *Summa Theologica*, likewise con-

tains chapters entitled "Touch," "Glances," etc., yet is silent on the subject here mentioned, whereas it says, concerning the *tactus inhonestus bestiarum* (indecent touching of animals): "It must be judged according to the intention and condition of the person touching" (p.291).

49. II, II, 141, 4 ad 3; cf. also Mal. 8, 1 ad 9

50. I, 5, 4 ad 1

51. *Ratio imitatur naturam* (reason imitates nature) I, 60, 5. "Since those things which are according to nature, have been ordered by Divine reason, which human reason ought to imitate, whatever is done according to human reason which is against the order commonly found in natural things, is defective (*vitiosum*) and a sin." II, II, 130, 1. Cf. also II, II, 133, 1; Car. 1

52. In II Cor. 4, 5; cf. In Rom. 7, 4; C.G. 1, 20

53. *De oratione* 22

54. *De pudicitia* 1

55. *De spectaculis* 24

56. II, II, 8, 7

57. The passage runs as follows: "Be strict, then, in taking them to task, so that they may be soundly established in the faith, instead of paying attention to these Jewish fables, these rules laid down for them by human teachers who will not look steadily at the truth. As if anything could be unclean for those who have clean hearts! But for these men, defiled as they are by want of faith, everything is unclean; defilement has entered their very thought, their very consciences. They profess recognition of God, but their practice contradicts it. . ." Titus I: 13-16.

58. II, II, 142, 2 ad 2; 142, 3

59. II, II, 141, 8 ad 3

60. *Omne peccatum formaliter consistit in aversione a Deo* (Every sin consists formally in a turn away from God). II, II, 10, 3; 148, 5 ad 2

61. Adam, *op. cit.*, p. 110

62. II, II, 20, 3

63. II, II, 154, 3 ad 1

64. Cf. Adam, *op. cit.*, p. 210
65. II, II, 154, 3 ad 1 (cf. also the objection that goes with this); II, II, 150, 3 ad 1
66. II, II, 123, 12
67. II, II, 141, 8
68. It is only the theological virtues, prudence and justice, says St. Thomas, that "simply" direct man toward the good. II, II, 157, 4

III

1. II, II, 152, 3; 152, 3 ad 5
2. St. Augustine, *De virginitate* 8
3. II, II, 152, 3; 152, 3 ad 1; 152, 5
4. ". . . that, whereas no forbiddance has diminished the honorable state of marriage and the nuptial benediction abides upon Holy Matrimony, there might nonetheless exist more exalted souls, who would disdain the married state as far as the physical union of man and wife is concerned, yet desire the sacrament, nor would imitate what is done in marriage, but would love that which is designated for marriage." *Pontificale Romanum, De benedictione et consecratione virginum* (On the Blessing and Consecration of Virgins)
5. Quoted in an essay by Maria Schlüter-Hermkes on St. Catherine of Genoa in *Die Christliche Frau*, 1924
6. The title of the first chapter of the *De perfectione vitae spiritualis* reads: "That the perfection of spiritual life is attained simply according to the love of God."
7. *De bono conjugali* 22
8. *De virginitate* 44
9. II, II, 152, 2, obj. 1; 152, 4, obj. 2
10. II, II, 152, 2 ad 1
11. II, II, 152, 4

IV

1. II, II, 146, 1 ad 4
2. *Quaestiones evangeliorum;* quoted in II, II, 146, 1 ad 2
3. II, II, 147, 3

4. Ibid.

5. II, II, 146, 1 ad 4

6. Quol. 5, 18

7. II, II, 146, 1 ad 2

8. II, II, 147, 1 ad 2

9. "In such a way, however, that thereby nature is not grievously burdened." II, II, 147, 7; cf. II, II, 147, 6

10. II, II, 147, 5 ad 3

11. II, II, 150, 1 ad 1

12. Quol. 5, 18

13. II, II, 148, 6; Mal. 14, 4

14. *Divine Comedy*, Purgatory XXIII, 31ff; Norton translation.

15. *Regula pastoralis* 3, 19

V

1. II, II, 141, 4

2. Ibid. It should be noted here that St. Thomas does not think that the sense of taste is only a special form of the sense of touch; cf. Mal. 14, 3 ad 4

3. Ver. 22, 5

4. I, 76, 5

5. In An. 8

6. Ibid.

7. In An. 3, 18

8. I, 76, 5

9. In An. 2, 19

10. I, 76, 5

11. In An. 2, 19; cf. An. 8

12. III, 15, 6; 26, 3 ad 9

13. *Blätter und Steine*, Hamburg, 1934, p. 171f.

14. II, II, 141, 6 ad 1

VI

1. Mal. 8, 2. "From all our goods we seek some excellence." I, II, 47, 2

2. II, II, 161, 6; 162, 3 ad 2

3. II, II, 161, 1 ad 3; 129, 3 ad 4

4. II, II, 162, 1 ad 3
5. II, II, 129, 1
6. II, II, 129, 3 ad 5
7. II, II, 129, 2
8. II, II, 129, 1 ad 3
9. II, II, 129, 2 ad 3
10. II, II, 129, 3 ad 4
11. Ibid.
12. II, II, 129, 4 ad 2
13. II, II, 129, 3 ad 5
14. II, II, 129, 4 ad 2
15. II, II, 129, 6
16. II, II, 129, 7
17. II, II, 129, 7 sed contra
18. Johannes Cassianus, *De coenob. instit.* 12, 7
19. II, II, 162, 5; 161, 1 ad 5; 161, 2 ad 3; 161, 6
20. II, II, 161, 3 ad 3
21. II, II, 161, 3
22. Cf. Brother Leo, *Mirror of Perfection,* chap. LXI
23. *Epist. ad Januarium* 54, 4

VII

1. I, II, 23, 1 ad 1
2. *Ad invadendum malum laesivum.* I, II, 23, 3
3. I, 81, 2
4. Mal. 12, 1
5. II, II, 158, 1
6. "To act from passion diminishes both honor and reproach, but to act *with* passion can increase both." Ver. 26, 7 ad 1
7. *Moralia* in Job 5: 45
8. II, II, 158, 1 ad 2; cf. Mal. 12, 1 ad 4
9. II, II, 158, 5
10. II, II, 157, 4 ad 1
11. *Tumor mentis.* Mal. 12, 5
12. II, II, 157, 1
13. II, II, 157, 4
14. II, II, 158, 8; Mal. 12, 5 ad 3

15. II, II, 156, 4
16. II, II, 158, 4
17. II, II, 35, 1 ad 4
18. Ver. 24, 10

VIII

1. *Confessions* 10, 35
2. II, II, 166, 2 ad 3
3. II, II, 167, 1 ad 3
4. *Sprüche in Prosa*
5. II, II, 167, 1
6. *Confessions* 10, 35
7. *De vera religione* 53
8. 2nd ed., Halle, 1929, p. 172
9. Cf. Josef Pieper, *Über die Hoffnung*, 2nd ed., Leipzig, 1938, p. 55 ff.
10. Mal. 11, 4
11. II, II, 35, 3 ad 3
12. *Sein und Zeit*, p. 173

IX

1. II, II, 142, 4
2. II, II, 153, 5 ad 2
3. II, II, 142, 2
4. II, II, 142, 4; 151, 4 ad 2
5. II, II, 153, 5 ad 2. St. Thomas here quotes Scripture: "Dalliance and wine and revelry . . . steal away your wits." Osee 4: 11
6. Dogmatic decision of the Council of Vienne (1311 to 1312); cf. Denziger, *Enchiridion symbolorum*, 481
7. II, II, 161, 6 ad 2
8. Cf. Josef Pieper, *Über die Hoffnung*, p. 49ff.
9. Cf. also Mal. 15, 4 ad 3; II, II, 153, 4 ad 2
10. *Collationes patrum* 1, 4
11. *De moribus Ecclesiae* 15
12. *Poetics* 6, 2 (1449b)
13. II, II, 141, 1 ad 3